Evaluating Medical Treatment Guideline Sets for Injured Workers in California

T0308385

Teryl K. Nuckols, Barbara O. Wynn, Yee-Wei Lim, Rebecca N. Shaw,
Soeren Mattke, Thomas Wickizer, Philip Harber, Peggy Wallace,
Steven M. Asch, Catherine MacLean, Rena Hasenfeld Garland

Prepared for the Commission on Health and Safety and Workers' Compensation and
the Division of Workers' Compensation, California Department of Industrial Relations

INSTITUTE FOR CIVIL JUSTICE
and RAND HEALTH

The research described in this report was conducted by the RAND Institute for Civil Justice and RAND Health, units of the RAND Corporation. This research was sponsored by the Commission on Health and Safety and Workers' Compensation and the Division of Workers' Compensation, California Department of Industrial Relations.

Library of Congress Cataloging-in-Publication Data

Evaluating medical treatment guideline sets for injured workers in California / Teryl K. Nuckols ... [et al.].
    p. cm.
    "MG-400."
    Includes bibliographical references.
    ISBN 0-8330-3835-4 (pbk. : alk. paper)
    1. Workers' compensation—Law and legislation—California. 2. Disability evaluation—Law and legislation—California. 3. Insurance, Disability—Medical examinations—California. I. Nuckols, Teryl K. II. Rand Corporation.

KFC592.E93 2005
344.79402'18—dc22

                                 2005020346

The RAND Corporation is a nonprofit research organization providing objective analysis and effective solutions that address the challenges facing the public and private sectors around the world. RAND's publications do not necessarily reflect the opinions of its research clients and sponsors.

RAND® is a registered trademark.

Published 2005 by the RAND Corporation
1776 Main Street, P.O. Box 2138, Santa Monica, CA 90407-2138
1200 South Hayes Street, Arlington, VA 22202-5050
201 North Craig Street, Suite 202, Pittsburgh, PA 15213-1516
RAND URL: http://www.rand.org/
To order RAND documents or to obtain additional information, contact
Distribution Services: Telephone: (310) 451-7002;
Fax: (310) 451-6915; Email: order@rand.org

Preface

This report presents an examination of the medical guidelines that might be used to evaluate the appropriateness of care provided California's injured workers, based on the following requirements in California Senate Bill 228 [Alarcón], enacted in September 2003:

- The Commission on Health and Safety and Workers' Compensation is to survey for nationally recognized evidence-based utilization guidelines and make recommendations to the Division of Workers' Compensation (DWC).
- The Administrative Director (AD) of DWC is to adopt by December 1, 2004, a utilization schedule that will set presumptive standards for the duration and scope of medically appropriate care.

The study, prepared by the RAND Institute for Civil Justice and RAND Health, units of the RAND Corporation, identifies comprehensive guideline sets addressing work-related injuries, evaluates their technical quality and clinical content, and highlights policy issues that should be considered in implementing them. The summary of this report is an abridged version of the study findings that should be of general interest to stakeholders in the California workers' compensation program. The text presents the full details of the guideline evaluation method, results, and implementation issues. It is intended as a reference for readers seeking more-detailed information on guidelines for the appropriateness of care provided to injured workers in California, and it may also be of interest to health-services researchers in other states.

This work was performed for the Commission on Health and Safety and Workers' Compensation and the Division of Workers' Compensation, California Department of Industrial Relations. It is part of a broader study of the cost and quality issues affecting medical care provided to injured workers in California and strategies to improve the quality and efficiency of that care. The findings of the other study tasks will be reported in separate documents.

Contents

Figures

Tables

Summary

Introduction

In recent years, the California workers' compensation system has been encumbered by rising costs and high utilization of medical care. Medical costs for injured workers grew by 111 percent between 1997 and 2002 and now represent more than half the total costs of workers' compensation (California Workers' Compensation Institute, 2004). Medical care payments were more than twice the national average in 2002 (National Academy of Social Insurance, 2004).

A comparative study across 12 states performed by the Workers' Compensation Research Institute concluded that California's higher medical costs resulted primarily from high utilization rather than high prices (Telles, Wang, and Tanabe, 2004). The study found that

- California had more visits per claim—in total and for physicians, chiropractors, and physical/occupational therapists—than any of the other states studied.
- The average number of visits for more-mature claims was 31 percent higher for hospitals, 70 percent higher for physicians, and 150 percent higher for chiropractors than the 12-state median.

To address these concerns, the California legislature passed a series of initiatives aimed at reducing costs and inappropriate medical care utilization in the system (AB 749 [Calderon], 2002; SB 228 [Alarcón], 2003; SB 899 [Poochigan], 2004). SB 228, passed in 2003, called for the adoption of medical treatment guidelines to define the appropriate utilization of medical care provided to injured workers, using the American College of Occupational and Environmental Medicine (ACOEM) guidelines as presumptively correct on an interim basis. Previously, physicians' treatment plans were presumed to be correct under the law. SB 899, passed in 2004, refined some of the requirements of SB 228. The study reported here, jointly sponsored by the California Commission on Health and Safety and Workers' Compensation (CHSWC) and the California Division of Workers Compensation (DWC), surveys and evaluates medical treatment guidelines for injured workers in California, as specified in the revised labor code (California Labor Code, 2004):

> §77.5(a): [CHSWC] shall conduct a survey and evaluation of evidence-based, peer-reviewed, nationally recognized standards of care.

> §5307.27: [The Administrative Director of DWC, in consultation with CHSWC, will adopt after public hearings] a medical treatment utilization schedule, that shall incorporate the evidence-based, peer-reviewed, nationally recognized standards of care . . . and that shall address, at a minimum, the frequency, duration, intensity, and appropriateness of all treatment procedures and modalities commonly performed in workers' compensation cases.

In calling for guidelines specifying the appropriate utilization of medical care, SB 228 required CHSWC to survey and evaluate existing medical treatment guidelines. Using the results of the evaluation, the state was to adopt either the ACOEM guidelines or a better alternative in the longer term. By December 1, 2004, in consultation with CHSWC, the Administrative Director (AD) of DWC was required to adopt a utilization schedule based on CHSWC's recommendations (SB 228 [Alarcón], 2003).

Developing Research Objectives

The legislation establishes a scientific basis for addressing medical care utilization in the California workers' compensation system. The phrase "evidence-based, peer-reviewed, nationally recognized standards of care" refers to the science of evidence-based medicine, which means using the best available research evidence to support medical professionals' decisionmaking (Sackett et al., 1996). The objective of evidence-based medicine has been defined as "minimizing the effects of bias in determining an optimal course of care" (Cohen, Stavri, and Hersh, 2004).

Medical treatment guidelines are an important tool for implementing evidence-based medicine. Guidelines are systematically developed statements that assist practitioner, patient, and, in this case, payor decisions about appropriate health care for specific clinical circumstances (Field and Lohr, 1990). A high-quality guideline can help curtail the effects of bias in formulating a treatment plan (AGREE Collaboration, 2001). Guidelines have many applications; perhaps the most common is distilling research evidence into a more usable form for busy clinicians. Insurers and third-party payors can also employ guidelines to determine whether a specific treatment is appropriate for a particular patient and therefore whether it should or should not be provided.

Techniques used by or on behalf of third-party payors to reduce health care costs by assessing the appropriateness of care provided to individual patients are collectively called *utilization management* (Gray and Field, 1989). There can be substantial variability in utilization management practices, particularly in the criteria used for assessing whether care is appropriate (Gray and Field, 1989; Wickizer and Lessler, 2002). Because a lack of standardization may affect access to and quality of care for patients, the recently passed workers' compensation legislation requires payors to employ review criteria that are consistent with the guidelines adopted by the state of California (California Labor Code, 2004).

To manage both the initial selection of treatment and the quantity of care provided, the adopted utilization schedule is required by SB 228 to address "frequency, duration, intensity, and appropriateness." Prior RAND researchers have defined appropriate medical care as care for which the potential benefits to the patient outweigh the potential risks, irrespective of cost. Inappropriate care is defined as care for which risks outweigh the potential benefits. Care of uncertain appropriateness falls between the two (Fitch et al., 2001). The current study used these existing definitions. The utilization schedule must also address, when relevant, frequency, intensity, and duration, i.e., quantity of care (SB 228 [Alarcón], 2003).

The legislation calls for guidelines addressing "all treatment procedures and modalities commonly performed in workers' compensation cases." Workers experience a broad range of injuries of the muscles, bones, and joints, as well as a wide variety of other medical problems. These often require diagnostic tests, such as X-rays and magnetic resonance imaging (MRI). In California, common therapies include medication, physical therapy, chiropractic manipulation, joint and soft-tissue injections, and surgical procedures.

To enable the state to manage medical utilization costs, the guidelines will have to address diagnostic tests and therapies that are not only common, but also costly, either individually or in the aggregate. Utilization management should be most cost-effective when it focuses on costly services (Wickizer, Lessler, and Franklin, 1999). Therefore, our analysis concentrated on diagnostic tests and therapies that are performed frequently and that contribute substantially to costs within the California workers' compensation system. We identified several such tests and therapies and consider them to be priority topic areas that the guidelines should cover: MRI of the spine, spinal injections, spinal surgeries, physical therapy, chiropractic manipulation, surgery for carpal tunnel and other nerve-compression syndromes, shoulder surgery, and knee surgery. Taken together, these procedures account for about 44 percent of the payments for professional services provided to California's injured workers. In addition, the surgeries account for about 40 percent of payments for inpatient hospital services.

Guideline Evaluation Methods and Findings

Our study identified and evaluated guidelines for these priority areas. We first identified guidelines for work-related injuries; we then screened those guidelines, using multiple criteria; finally, we conducted comparative evaluations of the selected guidelines. It is important to note that we accomplished these objectives in a very limited time frame and with limited resources; because of these constraints, we did not conduct an independent review of the clinical literature, nor did we develop guidelines ourselves.

Searching

We used the Institute of Medicine (IOM) definition of *guideline* as the basis for our search: "systematically developed statements to assist practitioner and patient decisions about appropriate health care for specific clinical circumstances" (Field and Lohr, 1990). We also included documents developed to assist payor decisions, because the legislation called for the guidelines to address utilization issues.

Using a variety of complementary sources, we identified 72 relevant guidelines. We searched the National Library of Medicine's MEDLINE and the National Guidelines Clearinghouse for practice guidelines published during the three years prior to June 2004, using keywords referring to work-related injuries. We surveyed the websites of relevant specialty society organizations listed by the American Medical Association (AMA). We contacted each of the other 49 U.S. states to inquire about workers' compensation guidelines, and we interviewed national and California workers' compensation experts, including providers, insurers, CHSWC and DWC staff, researchers, and our clinical panelists. We used Google to identify chiropractic guidelines and physical therapy guidelines, as well as to locate specialty society websites. We also posted a call for guidelines on the DWC website.

Screening

We next began the task of selecting guidelines that satisfy the requirements of the legislation and preferences of the state (the criteria are listed in Table S.1). In accordance with the legislation, our first selection criterion was that the guidelines must be evidence-based and peer-reviewed. Our second criterion was that the guidelines must be nationally recognized. We developed generous definitions for these criteria in order to be inclusive at this stage. Together, *evidence-based* and *peer-reviewed* were taken to mean based, at a minimum, on a systematic review of literature published in medical journals included in MEDLINE. Systematic reviews of the literature are standard and essential features of an evidence-based guideline development process, as reflected by the fact that they are required by the National Guidelines Clearinghouse and are included in various guideline-assessment methodologies (AGREE

Table S.1
Screening Criteria for Guidelines Warranting Further Evaluation

Evidence-based, peer-reviewed

Nationally recognized

Address common and costly tests and therapies for injuries of spine, arm, and leg

Reviewed or updated at least every three years

Developed by a multidisciplinary clinical team

Cost less than $500 per individual user in California

Collaboration, 2001; National Guidelines Clearinghouse, 2004; Shaneyfelt, Mayo-Smith, and Rothwangl, 1999). *Nationally recognized* was taken to mean any one of the following: accepted by the National Guidelines Clearinghouse; published in a peer-reviewed U.S. medical journal; developed, endorsed, or disseminated by an organization based in two or more U.S. states; currently used by one or more U.S. state governments; or in wide use in two or more U.S. states.

The remaining criteria were developed in conjunction with CHSWC and DWC. Our third criterion was that guidelines must address, to at least a minimal degree, common and costly tests and therapies for injuries of the spine, arm, and leg. To address these tests and therapies, the state could (1) choose to have a universe of multiple acceptable guidelines addressing each topic; (2) choose the single best guideline for each topic, putting multiple guidelines together into a patchwork; or (3) choose one guideline set that addresses most or all of the topics. A universe of multiple guidelines would provide the most flexible decisionmaking for clinicians, whereas a patchwork would enable the state to choose the single highest-quality guideline for each topic and to expand the number of topics addressed.

We chose to evaluate sets of guidelines rather than multiple individual guidelines, for several reasons. Multiple guidelines may vary in rigor of development and frequency of updating. Moreover, they may address the same injuries and treatments and make contradictory recommendations, which could foster litigation. This is especially problematic for patients with multiple injuries, who might be subject to several different guidelines at the same time. Finally, multiple guidelines may be more complex for the state to implement and administer and may be costly to users. Of course, some of these problems could affect sets of guidelines as well, and the content within each set may vary in quality.

In hopes of identifying a single guideline set that would address many common and costly work-related injuries in a rigorous, evidence-based fashion and would also facilitate implementation, we decided to pursue the guideline-set approach at this point in time. The short timeline on this project precluded us from pursuing both this approach and the patchwork approach simultaneously. If no acceptable guideline sets could be identified, the state would have the option of considering alternative strategies in the future.

Our fourth selection criterion was that the guideline sets be reviewed at least every three years. This requirement was based on prior RAND research demonstrating that new research evidence renders about 50 percent of guidelines out of date after 5.8 years and at least 10 percent out of date after 3.6 years (Shekelle et al., 2001).

Our fifth criterion was that multidisciplinary clinical panels had to be involved in developing the guidelines. A 1990 IOM report on clinical practice guidelines considered a multidisciplinary development process to be an important component of guideline quality. The report asserted that use of a multidisciplinary team increases the likelihood that (1) all relevant scientific evidence will be considered, (2) practical problems with using the guidelines will be identified and addressed, and (3) affected [provider] groups will see the guidelines as credible and will cooperate in implementing them (Field and Lohr, 1990). Accepted guideline-assessment tools share the requirement for a multidisciplinary development process (AGREE Collaboration, 2001; Shaneyfelt, Mayo-Smith, and Rothwangl, 1999). Also, studies suggest that multidisciplinary panels produce more-balanced interpretations of the literature than single-specialty panels do (Coulter, Adams, and Skelelle, 1995). Finally, we believe that sets of guidelines addressing diverse therapies and injuries should have input from a variety of relevant experts.

Our sixth criterion was that guideline sets must cost less than $500 per individual user. Some proprietary guidelines addressing work-related injuries are marketed predominantly to institutional users, such as insurers. In California, potential users of the workers' compensation medical treatment schedule also include providers, attorneys, judges, and many other types of individual users. We selected this threshold to ensure that evaluated guidelines would ultimately be available to individual as well as institutional users.

The following five guideline sets met all the screening criteria:

1. AAOS—Clinical Guidelines by the American Academy of Orthopedic Surgeons
2. ACOEM—American College of Occupational and Environmental Medicine Occupational Medicine Practice Guidelines
3. Intracorp—Optimal Treatment Guidelines, part of Intracorp Clinical Guidelines Tool®
4. McKesson—McKesson/InterQual Care Management Criteria and Clinical Evidence Summaries
5. ODG—Official Disability Guidelines: Treatment in Workers' Comp, by Work-Loss Data Institute

Many guidelines were eliminated because they did not address most of the cost-driver tests and therapies to at least a minimal degree. A few specialty society documents were excluded because they did not meet our definition of a guideline. Several state guidelines and specialty society guidelines were eliminated because their content was out of date or because we could not confirm an updating plan. No guidelines were eliminated solely for lack of a multidisciplinary panel or on the basis of cost.

Evaluating

The final step in our process was a comparative evaluation of the five selected guidelines, addressing both technical quality and clinical content. The technical quality evaluation assessed the process by which guidelines were developed and other dimensions. Although there are formal, accepted methods for developing guidelines, there is tremendous variation in the rigor of this process. We planned to exclude from further evaluation guidelines that performed especially poorly on technical quality. The clinical content evaluation assessed how well the guidelines address utilization decisions, i.e., appropriateness and quantity of treatment.

We evaluated technical quality with the AGREE instrument, which has been endorsed by the World Health Organization (WHO) and is becoming an accepted standard for guideline development (Grol, Cluzeau, and Burgers, 2003). AGREE addresses six domains that suggest an unbiased guideline (AGREE Collaboration, 2001):

1. **Scope and purpose:** whether the overall objective, clinical questions, and target patients are specifically described.
2. **Stakeholder involvement:** whether the developers had input from all the relevant professional groups, sought patients' preferences, and piloted the guideline among defined target users.
3. **Rigor of development:** whether developers used systematic and explicit methods to search for evidence and formulate recommendations, considered potential health benefits and risks, had the guideline externally reviewed, and provided an updating plan.
4. **Clarity and presentation:** whether the guideline makes specific and unambiguous recommendations, presents management options clearly, and includes application tools.
5. **Applicability:** whether developers considered organizational barriers and costs of applying the guideline and provided key review criteria for monitoring implementation.
6. **Editorial independence:** whether the guideline is editorially independent from the funding body and conflicts of interest of guideline development members have been recorded.

The RAND team rated the guideline sets on these domains, using the guidelines themselves as well as detailed descriptions and corroborating evidence provided by guideline developers.

All five of the selected guideline sets performed reasonably well in the technical evaluation, which produced standardized domain scores ranging from 0.00 (lowest) to 1.00 (highest) (Table S.2). *Scope and purpose* were well defined for all. *Stakeholder involvement* was weakest for AAOS, strongest for McKesson, and good for the rest. *Rigor of development* was very good for all. *Clarity and presentation* were excellent for all. *Applicability* was variable because developers often neglected implementation—McKesson was good, ODG was better, and the others were poor. *Editorial independence* was lowest for Intracorp and excellent for the rest.

Two prior studies that evaluated a total of about 150 guidelines found highly variable scores across all six domains (Burgers et al., 2004; Harpole et al., 2003). Our five selected guideline sets scored higher in the *rigor of development* and *editorial independence* domains than many guidelines did in other studies. Like guidelines from other studies, our five guidelines were relatively weak in the *stakeholder involvement* and *applicability* domains. Overall, the scores of our five guidelines were higher than those in the two prior studies, probably because we included additional details provided by guideline developers. Because all five of these guidelines did reasonably well in the technical quality evaluation, we decided none warranted elimination on this basis.

Next, a multidisciplinary clinical panel evaluated guideline content, assessing relevant content within each guideline and considering ten selected therapies in slightly greater detail. Relevant content addressed utilization decisions—specifically, appropriateness of care and quantity of care. We believe that, to be useful in making utilization decisions, the relevant content should be comprehensive (applicable to most patients) and valid (consistent with evidence or expert opinion). Panelists rated guidelines independently, then met to discuss areas of disagreement and to re-rate the guidelines.

For our panel, we selected 11 clinicians referred by national specialty societies. We sought national experts in musculoskeletal injuries who were practicing at least 20 percent of the time and who had some experience treating injured workers. Eight

Table S.2
Technical Quality Evaluation—AGREE Instrument Results
(Standardized Domain Scores)

Domain	AAOS	ACOEM	Intracorp	McKesson	ODG
Scope and purpose	1.00	0.89	0.89	1.00	1.00
Stakeholder involvement	0.54	0.79	0.79	0.88	0.79
Rigor of development	0.81	0.88	0.83	0.88	0.81
Clarity and presentation	0.96	0.88	1.00	1.00	0.96
Applicability	0.17	0.33	0.33	0.61	0.72
Editorial independence	1.00	1.00	0.75	1.00	0.92

national societies, representing a broad spectrum of providers caring for injured workers, made nominations. The only desired specialty that was not represented among our nominees was radiology. We selected clinical leaders from a diversity of geographic locations and practice settings, with diverse experience in caring for injured workers. To avoid potential conflicts of interest, we wanted no more than about 20 percent of the selected panelists to be from California, and we would have excluded panelists involved in the development of the guidelines under review. We gave preference to individuals experienced in the development, evaluation, or implementation of medical treatment guidelines, and experience with expert panels was a plus. To increase the discussion related to services not commonly ordered or provided by other panel members, we included two panelists expert in these services. We interviewed the most promising candidates by telephone to clarify their experience, and we contacted references to explore the ability of the candidates to function in groups. The final panel included one general internal medicine physician, two occupational medicine physicians, one physical medicine and rehabilitation physician, one physical therapist, one neurologist who is also board-certified in pain management, two doctors of chiropractic medicine, two orthopedic surgeons, and one neurosurgeon.

Panelists reviewed each guideline set in its entirety and evaluated ten selected therapies in detail: physical therapy, chiropractic manipulation, surgical decompression procedures, and surgical fusion procedures for lumbar spine problems; physical therapy, chiropractic manipulation, and surgery for carpal tunnel syndrome; physical therapy, chiropractic manipulation, and surgery for shoulder injuries. We selected therapies representing regions of the body frequently injured at work, such the spine and the large and medium-sized joints in the arms and legs. Within each category, we focused on cost-driver tests and therapies, preferring those for which the guidelines had different recommendations and for which we had panel nominees providing the services addressed. Our limited time frame forced us to narrow the number of topics under consideration. Because all of the guidelines made similar recommendations about spinal MRI and knee surgery, there seemed little benefit to comparing these topics. Furthermore, the lack of a radiologist on the panel would have made it difficult to evaluate MRI of the spine or spinal injections. This left us with the ten therapies listed above, which included surgery and physical modalities, i.e., physical therapy and chiropractic manipulation. We needed to distinguish between physical therapy and chiropractic manipulation because we did not want panelists to rate the same content twice. California chiropractors told us that there is some overlap between the physical modalities provided by these two specialties and that the appropriateness of manipulation influences chiropractors' decisions to provide other physical modalities. We therefore defined physical therapy as treatments provided by physical therapists and chiropractic manipulation as any additional treatments that can be provided only by chiropractors.

Although the residual (i.e., nonselected) content within each guideline varied in scope, we wanted to evaluate such content. Panelists rated residual content in each guideline as though it were a separate topic, considering other common and costly therapies for work-related injuries. Panelists also evaluated the entire content of each guideline, considering common and costly therapies for work-related injuries. They then rated and ranked the guidelines.

To facilitate rating, we provided the panelists with booklets containing relevant guideline chapters for the ten selected therapies, annotated to identify content addressing surgery, physical therapy, and chiropractic manipulation. For the residual- and entire-content evaluations, each panelist was provided with electronic access to the entire content of the five guidelines.

Because we identified no existing methods for rating the clinical content of guidelines, we adapted the RAND/UCLA Appropriateness Method (RAM), having panelists rate guideline comprehensiveness and validity for each of the various topics. Panelists rated comprehensiveness and validity separately on nine-point scales, with 9 as the highest rating. Panelists who were unfamiliar with a topic were instructed to rate the content a 5 (Fitch et al., 2001).

In the analysis, ratings were interpreted as follows:

- Comprehensive or valid: a median rating of 7 to 9 without disagreement.
- Not comprehensive or invalid: a median rating of 1 to 3 without disagreement.
- Uncertain comprehensiveness or validity: a median rating of 4 to 6, or any rating with disagreement.

After the panelists ranked the entire content of each guideline, we determined its median rank.

Using these methods, we found that the appropriateness of particular kinds of surgery is addressed well by the various guideline sets, as shown in Table S.3. In the table, *Yes* means the panel agreed that the content was both comprehensive and valid. *Not comprehensive* means the panel agreed that the guideline was not comprehensive; we assume minimal relevant content and do not report validity. *Not valid* means that the content was of uncertain or better comprehensiveness, and the panel agreed that the content was not valid. *Validity uncertain* means that the content was of uncertain or better comprehensiveness and the panelists were uncertain of validity.

Panelists agreed that the AAOS guideline set was valid and comprehensive for lumbar spinal decompression and fusion surgeries. They were uncertain whether it was valid for carpal tunnel surgery and agreed that it was not comprehensive in addressing shoulder surgery. Panelists agreed that the ACOEM guideline was valid and comprehensive for lumbar spinal decompression surgery, carpal tunnel surgery, and shoulder surgery. Validity was uncertain for lumbar spinal fusion surgery. Panelists

Table S.3
Panelists' Assessment of the Comprehensiveness and Validity of Content Addressing the Appropriateness of Surgical Procedures

	AAOS	ACOEM	Intracorp	McKesson	ODG
Lumbar spinal decompression	Yes	Yes	Validity uncertain	Yes	Validity uncertain
Lumbar spinal fusion	Yes	Validity uncertain	Not valid	Validity uncertain	Validity uncertain
Carpal tunnel surgery	Validity uncertain	Yes	Validity uncertain	Yes	Yes
Shoulder surgery	Not com-prehensve	Yes	Yes	Yes	Yes

agreed that the Intracorp guideline was valid and comprehensive for shoulder surgery and invalid for lumbar spinal fusion surgery; the other two topics were of uncertain validity. The McKesson guidelines for surgical topics were rated the same as the ACOEM guidelines. The ODG guideline set was rated comprehensive and valid for both carpal tunnel surgery and shoulder surgery; the other two topics were of uncertain validity.

As shown in Table S.4, appropriateness of physical modalities is rarely addressed well by any of the five guidelines. Panelists were uncertain of the validity of the AAOS guideline for two topics and agreed that it was not comprehensive for the four others. Panelists agreed that the ACOEM guideline was valid and comprehensive for physical therapy of the shoulder. They agreed that it was not comprehensive for chiropractic manipulation of the shoulder. Validity was uncertain for the other four topics. Panelists agreed that the Intracorp guideline was not valid for chiropractic manipulation of the spine and carpal tunnel. Validity was uncertain for the remain-

Table S.4
Panelists' Assessment of the Comprehensiveness and Validity of Content Addressing the Appropriateness of Physical Modalities

	AAOS	ACOEM	Intracorp	McKesson	ODG
Lumbar spine physical therapy	Validity uncertain	Validity uncertain	Validity uncertain	Validity uncertain	Validity uncertain
Lumbar spine chiropractic	Not compre-hensive	Validity uncertain	Not valid	Validity uncertain	Validity uncertain
Carpal tunnel physical therapy	Not compre-hensive	Validity uncertain	Validity uncertain	Validity uncertain	Yes
Carpal tunnel chiropractic	Not compre-hensive	Validity uncertain	Not valid	Yes	Yes
Shoulder physical therapy	Validity uncertain	Yes	Validity uncertain	Yes	Validity uncertain
Shoulder chiropractic	Not compre-hensive	Not compre-hensive	Validity uncertain	Not compre-hensive	Not compre-hensive

ing topics. They agreed that the McKesson guideline was valid and comprehensive for chiropractic manipulation of the carpal tunnel and physical therapy of the shoulder. They also agreed that it was not comprehensive in addressing chiropractic manipulation of the shoulder. Validity was uncertain for the other three topics. Panelists agreed that the ODG guideline was valid and comprehensive for physical therapy and chiropractic manipulation of the carpal tunnel. They agreed that it was not comprehensive in addressing chiropractic manipulation of the shoulder. Validity was uncertain for the other three topics.

Quantity of physical modalities is rarely addressed well by any of the five guidelines, as is evident from Table S.5. Panelists agreed that the AAOS guideline was not comprehensive in addressing the six quantity topics. They agreed that the ACOEM guideline was valid and comprehensive for physical therapy of the carpal tunnel. They agreed that it was valid for physical therapy of the shoulder but were uncertain of its comprehensiveness. Validity was uncertain for physical therapy of the spine. Panelists agreed that it was not comprehensive for the remaining three topics. Panelists agreed that the Intracorp guideline was not valid for chiropractic manipulation of the spine and carpal tunnel. It was of uncertain validity for all physical therapy topics and for chiropractic manipulation of the shoulder. Panelists agreed that the McKesson guideline was comprehensive and valid for chiropractic manipulation of the carpal tunnel. They agreed that it was not comprehensive for chiropractic manipulation of the shoulder. Validity was uncertain for the remaining topics. They agreed that the ODG guideline was comprehensive and valid for physical therapy of the shoulder, and they agreed that it was not comprehensive for chiropractic manipulation of the shoulder. Validity was uncertain for the remaining topics.

Table S.5
Panelists' Assessment of the Comprehensiveness and Validity of Content Addressing the Quantity of Physical Modalities

	AAOS	ACOEM	Intracorp	McKesson	ODG
Lumbar spine physical therapy	Not comprehensive	Validity uncertain	Validity uncertain	Validity uncertain	Validity uncertain
Lumbar spine chiropractic	Not comprehensive	Not comprehensive	Not valid	Validity uncertain	Validity uncertain
Carpal tunnel physical therapy	Not comprehensive	Not comprehensive	Validity uncertain	Validity uncertain	Validity uncertain
Carpal tunnel chiropractic	Not comprehensive	**Yes**	Not valid	**Yes**	Validity uncertain
Shoulder physical therapy	Not comprehensive	**Valid**, comprehensiveness uncertain	Validity uncertain	Validity uncertain	**Yes**
Shoulder chiropractic	Not comprehensive	Not comprehensive	Validity uncertain	Not comprehensive	Not comprehensive

Table S.6 presents summary results for each guideline, reiterating the appropriateness ratings, then presenting the residual-content and entire-content evaluations. To summarize, the panel ratings indicate that the panelists thought all five guideline sets require substantial improvement. However, they preferred the ACOEM guidelines.

1. The AAOS guideline addressed appropriateness well for two of the four surgical topics and none of the six physical modality topics. Panelists agreed that the guideline had little residual content. In the entire-content rating, panelists agreed the guideline was valid but were uncertain whether it was comprehensive. It was ranked last.
2. The ACOEM guideline addressed appropriateness well for three of the four surgical topics and one of the six physical modalities. Panelists were uncertain whether the residual content was valid. In the entire-content rating, panelists agreed that the guideline was valid but were uncertain whether it was comprehensive. It was ranked first.
3. The Intracorp guideline addressed appropriateness well for one of the four surgical topics and none of the six physical modalities. Panelists were uncertain whether the residual content was valid. In the entire-content rating, panelists agreed that the guideline was not valid. It was ranked third.
4. The McKesson guideline addressed appropriateness well for three of the four surgical topics and two of the six physical modalities. In the residual-content and

Table S.6
Clinical Evaluation Summary: Panelists' Assessment of Comprehensiveness and Validity

	AAOS	ACOEM	Intracorp	McKesson	ODG
Appropriateness					
Surgery	2 of 4 topics	3 of 4 topics	1 of 4 topics	3 of 4 topics	2 of 4 topics
Physical therapy and chiropractic	0 of 6 topics	1 of 6 topics	0 of 6 topics	2 of 6 topics	2 of 6 topics
Residual Content					
	Not comprehensive	Validity uncertain	Validity uncertain	Validity uncertain	Validity uncertain
Entire Content					
Rating	**Valid**, comprehensiveness uncertain	**Valid**, comprehensiveness uncertain	Not valid	Validity uncertain	Validity uncertain
Median rank	4	**1**	3	2	2

entire-content evaluations, panelists were uncertain of validity. This guideline set tied for second.

5. The ODG guideline addressed appropriateness well for two of the four surgical topics and two of the six physical modalities. In the residual-content and entire-content evaluations, panelists were uncertain of validity. This guideline set tied for second.

Panelists' qualitative comments and discussion tone and content during the meeting were informative in interpreting these results. They appeared quite comfortable rating the surgical topics, based on their personal understanding of the relevant literature. However, for the physical modalities, panelists providing those services and those not providing them had quite different understandings. Some of the physicians were relatively unfamiliar with certain physical modalities, such as chiropractic manipulation of the carpal tunnel and shoulder. Providers of physical modality services cited published literature for their specialties, and physicians occasionally admitted being unfamiliar with that literature. For some physical modality topics, it appears that little literature may exist at this time. For example, the two chiropractors on the panel, both very familiar with evidence-based medicine and chiropractic guidelines, were aware of only two preliminary studies addressing chiropractic manipulation for carpal tunnel syndrome.

At the conclusion of the meeting, panelists elaborated upon their ratings and preferences. Several panelists voiced the opinion that all five guidelines require substantial improvement. Seven of the 11 panelists felt that

- The five selected guidelines "are not as valid as everyone would want in a perfect world."
- "They do not meet or exceed standards; they barely meet standards."
- "California could do a lot better by starting from scratch."

Some panelists reported preferring the specialty society guidelines to the proprietary ones marketed for utilization management purposes, which they found too "proscriptive," meaning that the proprietary guidelines limited clinical options to a degree that made the panelists uncomfortable.

The panelists' comments may shed light on some internal inconsistencies in our findings. One notable inconsistency is that the ACOEM and McKesson guidelines performed similarly for the selected topics and for the residual content, yet the ACOEM was judged valid overall and the McKesson was not. When asked about this, some panelists explained that the McKesson guideline was overly proscriptive, as noted above. Clinicians may be biased against guidelines marketed for utilization management purposes or biased in favor of specialty society guidelines. Alternatively, the McKesson guideline may be overly proscriptive, limiting care options to an unacceptable degree.

Another inconsistency is the fact that all five guidelines did reasonably well in the technical quality evaluation, yet ratings were very uneven in the clinical content evaluation. This inconsistency was most pronounced for the physical modalities. There could be several possible explanations for this. First, even rigorously developed guidelines use expert opinion to fill gaps in the evidence. Such gaps appear common for physical modality issues, particularly quantity of care and chiropractic manipulation of the carpal tunnel. Panelists were less likely to agree that opinion-based recommendations are valid. Second, physicians might not know that chiropractors manipulate the extremities, making it difficult for them to develop or assess guidelines for such modalities. Third, although one would expect that good technical quality, including rigorous development methods, would produce valid clinical content, we know of no studies addressing this.

Our methods have important limitations that might also explain the inconsistencies. First, we were unable to provide panelists with literature reviews for the therapies under consideration. This is an especially important limitation for our evaluations of the physical modalities, because panelists understood this literature differently; and for chiropractic manipulation of the carpal tunnel, some panelists were not familiar with the relevant literature at all. Second, in typical RAND/UCLA appropriateness studies, panelists assess appropriateness for well-defined surgeries and categories of patients (Fitch et al., 2001). In contrast, we aggregated large amounts of clinical material and asked panelists to provide summary judgments. This may mean that panelists averaged highly valid content with invalid content, leading to intermediate, i.e., uncertain, summary judgments. The residual-content evaluation involved aggregating the largest amount of content; therefore, this weakness would be most pronounced in that evaluation. The residual content was rated of uncertain validity for four of the five guidelines. Third, to our knowledge, no methods for evaluating clinical content have been validated to date. We borrowed from validated methods to the degree possible, but the main premise of our evaluation, using an expert panel to assess and compare multiple guidelines, has not been described in the published literature.

Despite these limitations, the clinical content evaluation leads us to the following research conclusions. All five guideline sets appear far less than ideal—in the words of the panelists, they barely meet standards. The clinical panel preferred the ACOEM guideline to the alternatives and considered it valid but not comprehensive in the entire-content rating. The ACOEM guideline addresses cost-driver surgical topics and addresses them well for three of the four therapies the panel rated. A surgical weakness in the ACOEM guideline set, lumbar spinal fusion, is well addressed by the AAOS guideline set. The ACOEM guideline does not appear to address physical modalities in a comprehensive and valid fashion, but the other four guidelines do little better. The same is true of the residual content in each guideline.

Stakeholder Experiences and Insights

Since March 31, 2004, the ACOEM guideline has been implemented in the California workers' compensation system as presumptively correct on an interim basis. Through interviews with stakeholders, we learned about difficulties that have arisen during this period. Payors appear to be interpreting and applying the guideline inconsistently. Moreover, payors appear uncertain about which topics ACOEM covers in enough detail to determine appropriateness of care. Sometimes the guideline has been applied to topics that it addresses minimally or not at all, including chronic conditions, acupuncture, medical devices, home health care, durable medical equipment, and toxicology.

We received additional stakeholder input on the use of medical treatment guidelines within the California workers' compensation system after the clinical evaluation of the five guideline sets was completed. We invited selected stakeholders to a meeting, the purpose of which was twofold: to share our findings to date and to obtain their input on implementation issues. Most of the participants were representatives of stakeholder organizations that were suggested to us by CHSWC and represented a variety of perspectives: labor, applicants' attorneys, physicians and other practitioners, payors, and self-insured employers. Much of the meeting was spent on the issue of how the AD of DWC could address the topical areas in the ACOEM guidelines that need improvement.

A commonly shared viewpoint among the participants was that the longer-term goal should be to take the best guideline available for each topic area and patch these guidelines together into a single coherent set, but there were differing viewpoints on the mechanism for reaching that goal and the policies that should be adopted in the interim. Payors tended to favor "staying the course" until a more valid and comprehensive set could be developed. They noted that the ACOEM guidelines had just been implemented and that additional time was needed both to work out the issues with ACOEM and to consider carefully the consistency and administrative issues that might arise in using multiple guidelines. Other participants tended to favor using guidelines from different developers to address the shortcomings. They suggested different short-term strategies, ranging from using the AAOS guidelines for spinal surgery to adopting multiple guidelines for additional topical areas as long as they met some minimum criteria, such as listing in the National Guideline Clearinghouse or having been developed by the specialty societies. Longer-term strategies involved evaluating existing guidelines for other topical areas and working toward a comprehensive, consistent guideline set, using a multidisciplinary group of evaluators. These participants were concerned about the potential detrimental impact on workers of using guidelines with uncertain validity.

Because all of the comprehensive guideline sets we evaluated were of uneven quality, we agree with the common view among stakeholders that the state will need to patch multiple guidelines together into a coherent set. However, issues arise when multiple guidelines addressing the same topic are considered presumptively correct under the law. Identifying and resolving conflicting recommendations would therefore be helpful. Having a single high-quality guideline for each topic rather than multiple guidelines would probably minimize such conflicts.

On the basis of our research conclusions and the stakeholder comments described above, we make the following recommendations for the short term, the intermediate term, and the longer term.

Short Term (After December 1, 2004)

1. The panelists preferred the ACOEM guideline set to the alternatives, and this set is already in use in the California workers' compensation system; therefore, there is **no reason to switch to a different comprehensive guideline set at this time.**

2. ACOEM content was rated comprehensive and valid for three of the four surgical topics considered, and our evaluation methods appeared successful for these topics; therefore, **the state can confidently implement the ACOEM guidelines for carpal tunnel surgery, shoulder surgery, and lumbar spinal decompression surgery.**

3. Because spinal fusion surgery is especially controversial and risky, and its use is rapidly increasing in the United States (Deyo, Nachemson, and Mirza, 2004; Lipson, 2004), it warrants additional emphasis. The AAOS content was rated comprehensive and valid for this procedure and also for lumbar spinal decompression surgery. Therefore, **the state can confidently implement the AAOS guideline for lumbar spinal fusion surgery and, if convenient, for lumbar spinal decompression surgery.**

4. The ACOEM guideline set performed well for three of the four categories of surgery we evaluated. Generalizing these findings to other surgical topics would be reasonable; therefore, **the state could implement the ACOEM guideline for other surgical topics.**

5. We found the validity of the ACOEM guideline for the physical modalities and the remaining content uncertain, but our evaluation methods appeared to have important limitations for these areas; therefore, **we are not confident that the ACOEM guideline is valid for nonsurgical topics.** Deciding whether or not to continue using ACOEM for nonsurgical topics as an interim strategy remains a policy matter.

    a. We recommend that to identify high-quality guidelines for the nonsurgical topics, the state should proceed with the intermediate-term solutions described below as quickly as possible.

6. **We suggest implementing regulations to clarify the following:**

    a. Stakeholder interviews suggest that payors in the California workers' compensation system are applying the ACOEM guidelines inconsistently, sometimes for topics the guidelines do not address or address only minimally; therefore, **we recommend that the state issue regulations clarifying the topics for which the adopted guidelines should apply.**

       1. Our stakeholder interviews suggest that acupuncture, chronic conditions, and other topics may not be covered well by the ACOEM guideline.

    b. **For topics to which the adopted guideline does not apply, the state should clarify who bears the burden of proof for establishing appropriateness of care.**

    c. **For topics that are not covered by the adopted guideline and throughout the claims adjudication process, the state should consider testing the use of a defined hierarchy to weigh relative strengths of evidence.**

    d. Because the medical literature addressing appropriateness and quantity of care may be very limited for some physical modalities and other tests and therapies, some guideline content will include a component of expert opinion; therefore, **the state should clarify whether expert opinion constitutes an acceptable form of evidence** within "evidence-based, peer-reviewed, nationally recognized standards of care."

    e. Our stakeholder interviews suggest that payors are uncertain whether they have the authority to approve exceptions to the guidelines for patients with unusual medical needs. Therefore, **the state should consider specifically authorizing payors to use medical judgment in deciding whether care at variance with the adopted guidelines should be allowed.**

Intermediate Term

1. If the state wishes to develop a patchwork of guidelines addressing work-related injuries, our research suggests the following priority topic areas: **physical therapy of the spine and extremities, chiropractic manipulation of the spine and extremities, spinal and paraspinal injection procedures, MRI of the spine, chronic pain, occupational therapy, devices and new technologies, and acupuncture.**

    a. When guidelines within a patchwork have overlapping content, the state may want to identify and resolve conflicting recommendations before adopting the additional guidelines.

2. Because high scores in the technical evaluation were not associated with high evaluations by expert clinicians, **we recommend that future evaluations of existing medical treatment guidelines include a clinical evaluation component.**

Specifically, we recommend against adopting guidelines solely on the basis of acceptance by the National Guideline Clearinghouse or a similar standard because this ensures only technical quality.

3. If the state wishes to employ the clinical evaluation method we developed for multiple future analyses, **we suggest that at least one analysis should involve an attempt to confirm the validity of the clinical evaluation method,** including determining the effect of a literature review on panel findings.

4. Lack of a comprehensive literature review appeared to be a major limitation in our evaluation of content addressing the physical modalities; therefore, **future evaluations addressing the physical modalities should include a comprehensive literature review.**

Longer Term

1. Our technical evaluation revealed that ACOEM and AAOS developers did a poor job of considering implementation issues, and our stakeholder interviews indicated that payors are applying the ACOEM guideline in an inconsistent fashion. Therefore, **we recommend that the state develop a consistent set of utilization criteria (i.e., overuse criteria) to be used by all payors.**

   a. Rather than covering all aspects of care for a clinical problem, as guidelines do, the utilization criteria should be targeted to clinical circumstances relevant to determining the appropriateness of specific tests and therapies.

   b. Rather than defining appropriateness for all tests and therapies provided to injured workers, the criteria should focus on common injuries that frequently lead to costly and inappropriate services.

   c. The utilization criteria should be usable for either prospective or retrospective assessments of appropriateness, because utilization management in the California workers' compensation system involves both types of activities.

   d. The criteria should use precise language so that they will be interpreted consistently.

2. Another task within this project addresses developing a quality-monitoring system for California workers' compensation. Underuse of medical care is one important component of quality; therefore, the state may need to develop criteria for measuring underuse. **Developing the overuse and underuse criteria at the same time would be resource-efficient.**

3. There are two basic ways the state could develop overuse and underuse criteria:

   a. **The criteria could be developed from existing guidelines,** such as the ACOEM, AAOS, and any other guidelines judged valid in future studies. We suspect that it may be somewhat difficult to develop overuse criteria from clinical guidelines.

   b. **The criteria could be developed from the literature and expert opinion,** without the intermediate step of developing or selecting guidelines.

Acknowledgments

Funding for this work was provided by the California Commission for Health and Safety and Workers' Compensation (CHSWC) and the California Division of Workers' Compensation (DWC). We are extremely grateful for the valuable support and thoughtful guidance that we received throughout this study from our project officers: Christine Baker, Executive Director of CHSWC, and Anne Searcy, DWC Medical Unit. We also appreciate the time and energy provided by others at CHSWC, including Lachlan Taylor and Irina Nemirovsky.

We are indebted to our expert panelists who gave generously of their time, knowledge, and wisdom:

J. D. Bartleson, MD
Associate Professor of Neurology
Mayo Clinic College of Medicine
Rochester, MN

Edward Bernacki, MD, MPH
Associate Professor of Medicine and Environmental Health Sciences
Executive Director, Safety and Environment
Director, Division of Occupational Medicine
Johns Hopkins School of Medicine
Baltimore, MD

W. Benjamin Blackett, MD, FACS, JD
Neurosurgery Consulting
Tacoma, WA

Samuel Brown, PT
Clinical Professor, University of Kentucky
Clinical Professor, University of Louisville
President, Monticello Physical Therapy Services
Monticello, KY

Kim Christensen, DC, DACRB, CCSP, CSCS
Department of Rehabilitation & Wellness
Physical Medicine and Rehabilitation
PeaceHealth Hospital
Longview, WA

Stephen Hessl, MD, MPH
Director of Occupational Health
Occupational Health & Safety Clinic/DIA Clinic
Denver Health Medical Center
Denver, CO

John Leiner, MD
Associate Professor of Medicine,
Division of General Internal Medicine, Geriatrics, and Palliative Care
Director, Employee Health and Occupational Medicine Services
University of Virginia School of Medicine
Charlottesville, VA

Peter Mandell, MD
Assistant Clinical Professor of Orthopaedic Surgery,
University of California, San Francisco
Burlingame, CA

George McClelland, DC
Christiansburg, VA

Karl Sandin, MD
Central Coast Physical Medicine and Rehabilitation Group
Santa Barbara, CA

Richard Strain, Jr., MD
Memorial Hospital Regional, Memorial West Hospital, Jackson Memorial
   Hospital, and Hollywood Medical Center
Hollywood, FL

We thank the specialty societies that provided panelist nominations: the Society for General Internal Medicine, the American Academy of Physical Medicine and Rehabilitation, the American College of Occupational and Environmental Medicine, the American Physical Therapy Association, the American Chiropractic Association, the American Association of Neurological Surgeons, the American Academy of Neurology, and the American Academy of Orthopaedic Surgeons.

We are grateful to the many stakeholders and knowledgeable observers of the California workers' compensation system who shared their insights and experiences. We are also grateful for the thoughtful insights of RAND unit leaders, Robert Brook (RAND Health) and Robert Reville (RAND Institute for Civil Justice). We benefited greatly from the comments of Robert Harrison and Martin Shapiro on an earlier version of this document. Finally, we appreciate the tremendous efforts of Gustavia Clark, Christopher Dirks, Carole Gresenz, and Laura Zakaras, of the RAND staff, and Janet DeLand in bringing this effort to fruition in a timely manner.

Glossary

Appropriateness, appropriate medical care. An appropriate procedure [or modality] is one in which the expected health benefit (e.g., improved functional capacity, . . . increased life expectancy) exceeds the expected negative consequences [to the patient] (e.g., mortality, morbidity, . . . time lost from work) by a sufficiently wide margin that the procedure [or modality] is worth doing, exclusive of cost (Fitch et al., 2001).

Comprehensive guideline content. When referring to a particular type of test or therapy, the guideline addresses most patients who might be considered candidates for that test or therapy. When referring to a guideline set as a whole, the guidelines address the most common and costly types of treatments for work-related injuries.

Duration of therapy. The time interval over which a given procedure or modality is provided to a patient at a particular frequency or intensity.

Evidence-based guideline content. Consistent with published, peer-reviewed medical literature, ranked according to quality of evidence.

Evidence-based medicine. Using the best available evidence to support medical decision-making; the practice of using published, peer-reviewed medical literature to support diagnostic and therapeutic decisionmaking (Sackett et al., 1996).

Evidence-based, peer-reviewed guideline. Based, at a minimum, on a systematic review of literature published in medical journals included in the National Library of Medicine's MEDLINE.

Frequency of therapy. The number of procedures or modalities provided to a patient in a given time interval.

Guideline. Systematically developed statements that assist practitioner and patient decisions about appropriate health care for specific clinical circumstances (Field and Lohr, 1990). For this project, we added payor decisions.

Intensity of therapy. Medication dose or potency, the relative force exerted by or on a patient during physical modalities, and other measures quantifying a variably performed procedure or modality.

Multidisciplinary clinical team. A clinical team including at least three major types of providers who care for injured workers.

Nationally recognized. Accepted by the National Guideline Clearinghouse; published in a peer-reviewed U.S. medical journal; developed, endorsed, or disseminated by an organization based in two or more U.S. states; currently used by one or more U.S. state governments; or in wide use in two or more U.S. states.

Quantity of care. Frequency, intensity, or duration of a variably performed procedure or modality.

Systematic review. A review of a clearly formulated question that uses systematic and explicit methods to identify, select, and critically appraise relevant research and to collect and analyze data from the studies that are included in the review. Statistical methods may or may not be used to analyze and summarize the results of the included studies (Cochrane Reviewers' Handbook Glossary, 2003).

Utilization. Consumption of health care services.

Utilization management. A range of techniques used to manage health care costs by assessing the appropriateness or necessity of care provided to individual patients. Utilization management is performed by or on behalf of third-party payors and often attempts to reduce costs by preventing inappropriate or unnecessary care from being provided (Gray and Field, 1989; Wickizer and Lessler, 2002).

Utilization schedule. A guideline that can assist payor decisions about appropriate health care for specific clinical circumstances, particularly about limiting inappropriate care. The guideline should also address, when relevant, frequency, intensity, and duration, i.e., quantity of care (California Labor Code, November 2004).

Valid guideline content. Evidence-based or, in the absence of conclusive evidence, consistent with expert opinion.

CHAPTER ONE

Introduction

California workers' compensation is a complex system that provides medical care and wage-replacement benefits to injured workers. In recent years, the system has been characterized by rising medical costs, evidence of inappropriate utilization of medical care (overuse), and concerns about quality and satisfaction. Medical costs in California's workers' compensation system grew by 111 percent between 1997 and 2002 and now account for more than half of the costs to the system (California Workers' Compensation Institute, 2004). Medical benefit payments increased 26.3 percent in 2002 alone, compared with a national average increase of 9.4 percent, and medical care payments per 100,000 covered workers amounted to more than twice the national average (Williams, Reno, and Burton, 2004).

A comparative study across 12 states performed by the Workers' Compensation Research Institute concluded that California's higher medical costs resulted primarily from high utilization rather than high prices (Telles, Wang, and Tanabe, 2004). The study found that

- California had the highest number of visits per claim—in total and for physicians, chiropractors, and physical/occupational therapists—of any of the 12 states.
- The average number of visits for more-mature claims was 31 percent higher for hospitals, 70 percent higher for physicians, and 150 percent higher for chiropractors than the 12-state median.

Over the past decade, the California legislature has made several efforts to control the growth in workers' compensation costs. These include the implementation of the qualified-medical-examiner system, the requirement for signed perjury statements, the emphasis on health care organizations (HCOs) designated to provide care, and the requirement that physicians divest ancillary services to which they refer their patients (e.g., computed tomography (CAT) scanners and physical therapy services). While several of these efforts succeeded on a transient basis, they were ineffective in controlling the progressively rising costs.

To address these persistent concerns, the legislature recently passed a series of initiatives aimed at reducing costs and inappropriate medical care utilization in the system (AB 749 [Calderon], 2002; SB 228 [Alarcón], 2003; SB 899 [Poochigan], 2004). The approach called for in these initiatives centers on the use of medical treatment guidelines, i.e., systematically developed statements that assist decisions about appropriate health care for specific clinical circumstances (explained in further in Chapter Two) (Field and Lohr, 1990). Prior to this legislation, physicians' treatment plans were presumed to be correct under the law. SB 228, passed in 2003, adopted a temporary set of guidelines concerning treatment for injured workers; the guidelines were further defined in 2004 by SB 899. The temporary guidelines are those of the American College of Occupational and Environmental Medicine (ACOEM) (ACOEM, 2003), which remain the presumptively correct guideline unless and until the Administrative Director (AD) of the Division of Workers' Compensation (DWC) chooses to replace them.

The legislated plan is that, after suitable study and evaluation, either the ACOEM guideline set or a better alternative will be adopted in the longer term. The legislation calls for the AD of DWC to adopt a utilization schedule based on these guidelines by December 1, 2004. Its specific language requires that (California Labor Code, 2004):

> §77.5(a): [The Commission on Health and Safety and Workers' Compensation (CHSWC)] shall conduct a survey and evaluation of evidence-based, peer-reviewed, nationally recognized standards of care.

> §5307.27: [The Administrative Director of DWC, in consultation with CHSWC, will adopt, after public hearings,] a medical treatment utilization schedule, that shall incorporate the evidence-based, peer-reviewed, nationally recognized standards of care recommended by the Commission . . . and that shall address, at a minimum, the frequency, duration, intensity, and appropriateness of all treatment procedures and modalities commonly performed in workers' compensation cases.

To help address their legislative mandates, CHSWC and DWC jointly commissioned the RAND Corporation to conduct a study to inform their responses. This report presents the results of that study, the main goal of which was to identify and evaluate medical treatment guidelines that could be used as a basis for a utilization schedule for the California workers' compensation system. A secondary goal was to identify and analyze issues surrounding the implementation of a utilization schedule by payors and by the California legal system.

The legislation attempts to require a scientific basis for addressing medical care utilization in the California workers' compensation system. The phrase "evidence-based, peer-reviewed, nationally recognized standards of care" refers to the science of evidence-based medicine, which means using the best available research evidence to support medical professionals' decisionmaking (Sackett et al., 1996). The objective of evidence-based medicine has been defined as minimizing the effects of bias in determining an optimal course of care (Cohen, Stavri, and Hersh, 2004) (explained further in Chapter Two).

Medical treatment guidelines are an important tool for implementing evidence-based medicine. A high-quality guideline can help curtail the effects of bias in formulating a treatment plan (AGREE Collaboration, 2001). Guidelines have many applications, perhaps the most common of which is distilling research evidence into a more usable form for busy clinicians. Insurers and other organizations paying for medical care can also employ guidelines as a basis for determining whether a specific test or therapy is inappropriate for a particular patient and therefore should not be provided.

Techniques performed by or on behalf of third-party payors to reduce health care costs by assessing the appropriateness of care provided to individual patients are collectively called utilization management (Gray and Field, 1989) (also explained in Chapter Two). There is some evidence from a recent study that utilization management can reduce medical costs within workers' compensation systems (Wickizer, Lesser, and Franklin 1999). That study documented average savings of approximately $11,000 (1993 dollars) per denied unnecessary admission. The average saving from denying outpatient surgical care was approximately $4,000 per denied case. Because this utilization review program denied only a small number (<5 percent) of requests, aggregate savings were modest, on the order of $5 million for 9,000 claimants who were subject to review. Evidence from other studies also indicates the potential of utilization review to contain health care costs. Durable medical equipment is subject to significant overuse. A utilization review performed by a Blue Cross plan showed significant reductions in the use of this equipment and substantial cost savings (Wickizer, 1995).

There can be substantial variability in utilization management practices, particularly in terms of the criteria used for assessing whether care is appropriate (Gray and Field, 1989; Wickizer and Lessler, 2002). Because a lack of standardization may affect access to and quality of care for patients, recently passed legislation requires utilization management organizations to employ criteria that are consistent with the guidelines adopted by the state of California (California Labor Code, 2004). Although the legislation does not define the term, *utilization schedule* appears to mean medical treatment guidelines or utilization management criteria based on guidelines. To manage both the initial selection of therapy and the quantity of care provided, the legislation requires the guideline to address frequency, intensity, duration, and appropriateness (SB 228 [Alarcón], 2003).

The study reported here was undertaken to respond to the legislation calling for medical treatment guidelines addressing work-related injuries. Our understanding of the issues involved informed our approach. As described more fully below, the study consisted of several steps. First, we conducted a thorough search to identify potential guidelines. Second, we screened the identified guidelines on the basis of criteria required by the legislation and developed in conjunction with CHSWC and DWC. Third, we evaluated the guidelines that passed the screening criteria. The evaluation methods included technical evaluations by RAND staff and an evaluation by a national panel of expert clinicians. Fourth, we presented our findings to a panel of California stakeholders. Finally, by distributing this report, we are communicating our findings to CHSWC, DWC, and the public.

Chapter Two provides additional detail on background issues. and Chapters Three through Six explain our survey and evaluation methods and findings. Chapter Seven summarizes stakeholder experiences using ACOEM as the interim guideline set, as well as stakeholder comments on our results. Implementation issues for the future guidelines are discussed in Chapter Eight. Chapter Nine presents our analysis of the findings and recommendations for the short, intermediate, and longer term. Methodological details and complete results are given in the appendices.

CHAPTER TWO

Context

Policies Governing Medical Care in the California Workers' Compensation System

This section describes the legal code regulating the system by which injured workers receive medical care in California and explains important changes mandated by the recent legislation. The policies governing medical care in the California workers' compensation system both define the future uses of the medical treatment guidelines that will be adopted by the AD of DWC and raise questions regarding regulations that may facilitate the implementation of these guidelines for their multiple purposes.

The California Labor Code requires an employer to pay for all medical care reasonably required to cure or relieve the effects of a worker's injury or illness, with no deductibles or cost sharing required by the injured worker (L.C. §4600). Until recently, the care provided by the treating physician was "presumptively correct," meaning that injured workers were entitled to the care recommended by their treating physician.

Several features of the workers' compensation program, including the primary-treating-physician presumption, the worker's right to choose a primary treating physician after 30 days, and the lack of any cost-sharing obligations for the injured worker, are suspected of fueling the high utilization rates observed in California. A series of recent legislative changes repealed the primary-treating-physician presumption and established a new presumption of correctness that defines the therapies reasonably required to cure or relieve work-related injuries, based on medical treatment guidelines (AB 749 [Calderon], 2002; SB 228 [Alarcón], 2003; SB 899 [Poochigan], 2004). The Labor Code now stipulates that ACOEM's Practice Guidelines are "presumptively correct," thereby defining the therapies reasonably required to cure or relieve work-related injuries. The legislation requires the AD of DWC to eventually adopt a utilization schedule incorporating "evidence-based, peer-reviewed nationally recognized standards of care" addressing, "at a minimum, the frequency, duration, intensity, and appropriateness of all treatment procedures and modalities commonly performed in workers' compensation cases" (L.C. §5307.27).

The Role of the Primary Treating Physician

Historically, medical treatment in the California workers' compensation system has been predicated on the selection of a health care provider as the primary treating physician for an injured worker. The Labor Code allows chiropractors, acupuncturists, psychologists, optometrists, dentists, and podiatrists, as well as allopathic and osteopathic physicians, to serve as primary treating physicians. In addition, licensed nurse practitioners and physicians' assistants, while not qualifying as treating physicians, are permitted to perform various care functions, including providing medical treatment of a work-related injury in accordance with their authorized scope of practice. Other types of health care specialists (e.g., physical therapists, audiologists) may also provide care for injured workers, usually through referrals from the primary treating physician.

Until January 1, 2005, employers or their workers' compensation insurers were allowed to select the primary treating physician for treatment of work-related injuries or illness for the first 30 days after the condition was reported. After the first 30 days, employees were free to choose any qualified medical provider or facility for care of their condition. In January 1, 2005, new laws went into effect that allow employers or their workers' compensation insurers to create medical provider networks for treatment of injured workers. Under the new laws, employees of employers with medical provider networks are to use network providers throughout the course of their treatment.[1] For employers that do not use a medical provider network, the previous practice remains in effect.[2]

The Role of Medical Treatment Guidelines

In an effort to improve quality of care, the Industrial Medical Council (IMC) within the California Department of Industrial Relations (DIR) issued treatment guidelines for providers, giving them an analytical framework for the evaluation and treatment of common problems of injured workers. Developed in consultation with the medical community, these guidelines were intended to be educational and descriptive of generally accepted practices. According to the IMC regulations:

> These guidelines are intended to assure appropriate and necessary care for injured workers diagnosed with these types of industrial conditions. Due to many factors which must be considered when providing quality care, health care providers shall not be expected to always provide care within the stated guidelines. Treatment authorization, or payment for treatment, shall not be denied based solely on a health care provider's failure to adhere to the IMC guideline. These guidelines are not intended to be the basis for the imposition of civil liability or professional

---

[1] In this instance, *employer* means a self-insured employer, joint powers authority, or the state (LC §4616.5).

[2] Under certain circumstances, employees may predesignate a treating physician. Also, different requirements apply if an employer provides for medical treatment through an HCO.

sanctions. They are not intended to either replace a treating provider's clinical judgment or to establish a protocol for all patients with a particular condition. It is understood that some patients will not fit the clinical conditions contemplated by a guideline (California Code of Regulations, Title 8, Ch. 1, Art. 7, §70).

The recent legislative changes repealed the IMC guidelines, along with the treating-physician presumption. The Labor Code (§4600b) now stipulates that the ACOEM Practice Guidelines define therapies reasonably required to cure or relieve work-related injuries. The ACOEM guidelines are presumptively correct regarding the extent and scope of medical treatment regardless of the date of injury. The presumption affects the burden of proof required in legal situations and is rebuttable by "a preponderance of evidence establishing that a variance from the guidelines is reasonably required." For injuries not covered by the ACOEM guidelines, care is to be in accordance with "other evidence-based medical treatment guidelines recognized by the national medical community and that are scientifically based" (L.C. §4604.5(e)).

The ACOEM guidelines will be presumptively correct until the AD of DWC adopts a different guideline as the utilization schedule for California. The legislation calls for the AD, in consultation with CHSWC and after public hearings, to adopt such a utilization schedule by December 1, 2004. To provide the AD with a basis on which to select a utilization schedule, SB 899 requires CHSWC to conduct a survey and evaluation of "evidence-based, peer-reviewed nationally recognized standards of care" (L.C. §77.5). The utilization schedule ultimately adopted should incorporate the standards of care recommended by CHSWC and should address, "at a minimum, the frequency, duration, intensity, and appropriateness of all treatment procedures and modalities commonly performed in workers' compensation cases" (L.C. §5307.27).

The term *utilization schedule* does not have a commonly accepted definition. It is not clear whether the Labor Code intends that the nationally recognized evidence-based standards of care be issued as a utilization schedule in a one-step or two-step process. The new utilization schedule will be rebuttable by a "preponderance of scientific medical evidence establishing a variance from the guidelines" (L.C. §4604.5). With the term *scientific* added to the instruction, it appears that a higher standard may be required to rebut the utilization schedule than is required by the ACOEM guidelines.

Notwithstanding care determined by the ACOEM guidelines and those adopted by the AD as presumptively correct, the Labor Code now limits chiropractic care, occupational therapy, and physical therapy services to 24 visits each per industrial injury occurring on or after January 1, 2004, unless the employer authorizes additional visits in writing.

Implications for Utilization Management in California Workers' Compensation

Prior to the recent legislation, DWC regulations allowed employers (or insurers acting on their behalf) to establish a limited utilization review (UR) process. The regulations applied primarily to prospective requests for authorization of payment for treatment and required that the UR process use credible, physician-developed, medically based criteria. A comprehensive medical evaluation could be performed by an independent medical examiner if there was a dispute over the need for continuing medical treatment; however, if either the employer or the injured worker requested a hearing before a workers' compensation judge on whether the care was necessary, the primary-treating-physician presumption of correctness applied.

As revised by SB 228, the Labor Code now requires each employer, either directly or through its insurer, to have a UR process in place that may include prospective, concurrent, or retrospective review of medical care. While discretion is allowed regarding utilization management (UM) techniques, the UR process is to be governed by written policies and procedures that "ensure that decisions based on the medical necessity to cure and relieve" are consistent with the ACOEM guidelines (or the utilization schedule issued by the AD of DWC). Only a physician may modify, delay, or deny requests for authorization based on medical necessity (L.C. §4610). The Labor Code requires that the UR criteria be

- Developed with the involvement of practicing physicians
- Consistent with the ACOEM guidelines (or guidelines issued by the AD of DWC)
- Evaluated at least annually
- Disclosed to the physician and the employee if the criteria are used to modify care recommended by the treating physician
- Available to the public upon request

The administrative rules implementing the recent legislative changes in the UR process have been proposed but have not been implemented. A likely implementation issue will be the meaning accorded to the term *consistent* and whether the UR guidelines must be the same as the medical treatment guidelines or may be developed from those guidelines.

Implications for Disputes over Medical Treatment

Physicians who participate in the medical networks will be required to practice according to the ACOEM guidelines until the effective date of the utilization schedule issued by the AD. Thus, the standards of care incorporated into the guidelines may assume increased importance when the networks are established, since they may affect selection of participating physicians and how they practice. While an employee may challenge the diagnosis or therapy prescribed by the treating physician in the network by obtaining a second or third opinion within the network and an independent medical review provided by DWC, the guidelines are presumptively correct at each stage of the appeal. Thus, the Labor Code establishes a clear expectation that care furnished by providers in a medical network will be in accordance with the guidelines, which are intended to protect against both underuse and overuse. There are no explicit protections to assure that appropriate care is furnished to injured workers who have unusual medical needs not encompassed by the guidelines.

A hearing before a workers' compensation judge (whose decision may be appealed to the Workers' Compensation Appeals Board) is to be used to resolve disputes over the medical necessity of care furnished outside a medical network or HCO. An expedited hearing process is to be used to resolve issues involving concurrent care. As previously indicated, the guidelines are presumed correct during the appeals process. The Labor Code establishes the "preponderance of scientific medical evidence establishing a variance from the guidelines" as the burden of proof for rebutting the presumption (L.C. §4604.5).

SB 228 also establishes a second-opinion program for spinal surgery that is not explicitly linked to the guidelines. Disputed surgical recommendations are referred to a randomly selected qualified orthopedic surgeon or neurosurgeon for a second opinion. If the second opinion concurs with the treating physician's recommendation, the surgery is authorized. If the second opinion determines that the proposed surgery is not reasonably necessary, the parties proceed to an expedited hearing, in which case the guidelines are presumed correct.

In summary, the California Labor Code contemplates that the utilization schedule adopted by the AD will give concrete meaning to the requirement that injured workers receive care "reasonably required to cure and relieve the effects of a worker's injury or illness." At each stage of the process, from the treating physician in medical networks through the UR and appeal processes, the guidelines are presumed correct for defining medically necessary care. Addressing issues such as topical gaps in the guidelines and unusual cases will be important for assuring that California's injured workers have continued access to appropriate medical care. Chapter Eight highlights issues raised regarding the implementation of the ACOEM guidelines and discusses implementation policies that the AD may wish to consider.

Background on Evidence-Based Medicine, Medical Treatment Guidelines, and Utilization Management

The legislation discussed above calls for the incorporation of a scientific approach to addressing the problem of high medical care utilization in California workers' compensation. In requiring the use of "evidence-based, peer-reviewed, nationally recognized standards of care," the legislation rests on the science of evidence-based medicine and sanctions its implementation through the use of medical treatment guidelines. The legislature's efforts are intended to promote objective, unbiased decision-making by third-party payors and others as they determine the appropriateness of medical treatments provided to individual injured workers, i.e., as they manage the utilization of health care services.

This section describes the concepts of evidence-based medicine, medical treatment guidelines, and UM. Such concepts underlie our survey and evaluation of existing medical treatment guidelines; their strengths and limitations will ultimately shape the strengths and limitations of the "evidence-based, peer-reviewed, nationally recognized standards of care" adopted by the state.

Evidence-Based Medicine

Health care providers have historically decided which therapies may be effective for a particular patient by considering what has worked for similar patients in the past, drawing upon knowledge of physiology and anatomy, as well as anecdotes from a few prior patients. Today, clinical research, meaning the study of medical tests of therapies in living humans, enables providers to generalize from the experiences of numerous patients. Although basic science, experience, and intuition still play important, even irreplaceable, roles in medicine, physicians and other health care professionals are relying more and more upon evidence from clinical research studies to support their diagnostic and therapeutic choices. Within health care, this represents "a significant cultural shift, a move away from unexamined reliance on professional judgment toward more structured support and accountability for such judgment" (Field and Lohr, 1990).

Use of the best available evidence to support medical professionals' decision-making is often referred to as *evidence-based medicine* (Sackett et al., 1996), the objective of which has been defined as "to minimize the effects of bias in determining an optimal course of care" (Cohen, Stavri, and Hersh, 2004). Bias, meaning lack of objectivity and other factors that may distort conclusions, can exist at any stage in the medical decisionmaking process, from research through guideline development and clinical care.

There are many sources of bias in evaluating tests and therapies. Preconceived notions on the part of sponsors, researchers, and participants can influence the apparent efficacy of a therapy. Baseline patient characteristics, the natural course of illness, and chance may suggest an effect when there is none, or the absence of an effect when one exists. These problems can be alleviated by careful study design, particularly by the gold-standard design: the randomized controlled trial. In randomized controlled trials, participants are randomly assigned to receive either the therapy under study or a comparison therapy, which can be an accepted therapy or a placebo. While weaker designs can also mitigate bias, they often do so incompletely (Campbell and Stanley, 2005).

Once a research study is complete, its results must be made available to decisionmakers; this process, too, is subject to bias. Sponsors with a financial stake in a therapy have an incentive to discourage reporting of harm or ineffectiveness, and journal editors have a historical tendency to prefer studies showing positive effects of a therapy over those finding no benefit (De Angelis et al., 2004).

Evidence-based-medicine experts have developed formal processes to remedy the dual problems of weak study design and publication bias. Using these processes, researchers identify published and unpublished studies, then grade the evidence and compile it into summary conclusions. Three common approaches are Cochrane Collaboration reviews, other systematic reviews, and meta-analyses. Although bias can affect meta-analyses and systematic reviews (Miles et al., 2001), these are generally considered the highest-quality evidence that can be used to support medical decisionmaking. The widely accepted Agency for Health Care Policy and Research (AHCPR) hierarchy of evidence quality is shown in Table 2.1 (AHCPR, 1999).

Unfortunately, bias may also persist later in the clinical decisionmaking process. Despite their best efforts, practitioners can fall prey to inconsistency in the identification and application of evidence; therefore, many strategies have been developed to encourage and monitor the use of evidence-based care. Specialty societies and other organizations have developed medical treatment guidelines to standardize therapy and make important evidence readily available to busy clinicians. UM organizations sometimes use evidence-based guidelines to determine when practitioners are overusing inappropriate medical therapies. The study reported here focuses on two strategies for influencing provider behavior—medical treatment guidelines and UM programs—that, to varying degrees, incorporate evidence-based medical decisionmaking.

Although evidence-based medicine strives to bring objectivity to clinical decisionmaking, has widespread acceptance by clinicians, and has a broad range of applications, it has a critical drawback: Important clinical questions often remain inadequately addressed by high-quality research studies (Naylor, 1995; AHCPR, 1999).

Table 2.1
AHCPR Hierarchy of Evidence Quality

Rank	Level and Description
1a	Systematic review or meta-analysis of randomized controlled trials
1b	At least one randomized controlled trial
2a	At least one well-designed controlled study without randomization
2b	At least one well-designed quasi-experimental study, such as a cohort study
3	Well-designed nonexperimental descriptive studies, such as comparative studies, correlation studies, case-control studies, and case series
4	Expert committee reports or opinions and/or clinical experience of respected authorities

There are several possible reasons for this shortcoming, including rapid development of new therapies, research costs, and ethical and logistical obstacles. Private companies interested in demonstrating the efficacy of a patented therapy, such as a medication or device, and thereby realizing a financial return on a research investment often fund clinical trials. Because financial incentives are lacking for nonpatentable interventions, such as surgical procedures, exercises, and manual therapies, fewer trials address these interventions (AHCPR, 1999; Meltzer, 1998). Finally, ethical and logistical issues can constrain randomization, making high-quality trials infeasible and compelling researchers to resort to less-rigorous methods.

Unfortunately, evidence-based medicine offers little guidance for what to do when evidence is lacking or is of consistently poor quality (Jones and Sagar, 1995). One commentator notes, "When there are incomplete data or no available studies on new technologies, doctors are left to decide whether to take a minimal approach to treatment or to aggressively treat patients based on their own experience and beliefs" (Naylor, 1995). Much of the health care provided in the United States may lack relevant or high-quality evidence. Researchers have found that for three common, well-established procedures, from 5 to 32 percent of the care provided was of uncertain benefit to patients (Naylor, 1995; Park et al., 1989). The percentage is likely to be substantially higher for less-common and newer therapies.

Researchers have developed methods for addressing gaps in evidence, most of which involve having panels of expert clinicians formulate recommendations on the basis of experience. The AHCPR hierarchy includes expert opinion as a form of evidence, albeit the lowest form (AHCPR, 1999). Panels typically make opinion-based recommendations in the course of formulating evidence-based recommendations for related but different clinical questions. A variety of methods can be used to determine which opinions a panel formally endorses. Some methods force panelists to reach consensus, while others simply assess whether consensus exists naturally. The RAND/ UCLA Appropriateness Method (RAM) represents an example of the latter and has been in use for about 20 years (Fitch et al., 2001). Studies have demonstrated that two similarly composed expert panels will generally formulate similar recommendations when reviewing the same literature for a particular procedure, demonstrating that the panel method has moderate reliability (kappa statistics of about 0.5 to 0.7) (Shekelle, 2004; Shekelle, Chassin, and Park, 1998; Tobacman et al., 1999). In addition, the method has been found to predict the results of future randomized controlled trials quite reliably (Shekelle, Chassin, and Park, 1998).

In summary, *evidence-based medicine* means using the best available research evidence to support medical decisionmaking; its purpose is to make that decisionmaking as objective as possible. In evidence-based medicine, multiple strategies are used to ensure that the best evidence is communicated to and incorporated by clinicians as they determine an optimal course of care. However, evidence-based medicine has critical limitations; for example, it cannot assist decisionmaking in the absence of evidence, and such evidence is frequently lacking, although expert-panel methods can be used to fill gaps. For the California workers' compensation system, evidence-based medicine can provide a rational, unbiased framework for determining which therapies are appropriate, but it can do so only when high-quality research studies have addressed the therapies in question.

Medical Treatment Guidelines

Medical treatment guidelines have played an important role in the modern cultural shift toward evidence-based health care, facilitating evidence-based clinical decision-making and buttressing efforts to evaluate practitioner and health system performance. Guidelines have many applications, perhaps the most common of which is distilling research evidence into a more usable form for busy clinicians. A variety of HCOs use guidelines to increase the quality and consistency of the care provided to a particular group of patients or for a specific condition. Insurers and payors can employ UM guidelines to determine whether a particular service should be provided to a particular patient. Thus, according to the Institute of Medicine (IOM), medical treatment guidelines are "systematically developed statements that assist practitioner and patient decisions about appropriate health care for specific clinical circumstances" (Field and Lohr, 1990). In this study, we also include guidelines developed to assist payor decisions, because the California legislation calls for guidelines addressing utilization issues.

Specialty societies, state and federal agencies, health plans, provider groups, payors, and other organizations develop guidelines to outline preferred diagnostic and therapeutic approaches for typical patients with selected symptoms or diagnoses. Guidelines generally focus on a target population, such as injured workers, or a clinical problem, such as back pain. When focused on a certain population, guidelines may address a broad range of diagnostic and therapeutic decisions applicable to that population. When focused on a clinical problem, the guidelines may discuss a narrow range of decisions for a wider range of patients.

Thus, guidelines have defined objectives that lead them to focus on related clinical questions. Guideline developers attempt to answer questions that are clinically important in the management of the target population or problem. They formulate their recommendations on the basis of the highest-quality evidence available—usually meta-analyses, systematic reviews, and high-quality clinical trials. Where there are gaps in high-quality evidence, developers may bring in successively lower-quality evidence, including, when necessary, expert opinion. Many guidelines grade their recommendations according to the strength of supporting evidence, as described in Table 2.1 above, so that this is transparent to their users.

Despite the existence of formal, accepted methods for developing guidelines, there is tremendous variation in the rigor of this process (Shaneyfelt, Mayo-Smith, and Rothwangl, 1999). One important reason is the many potential sources of bias in guideline development. Some biases are the result of the limitations of evidence-based medicine, such as the lack of high-quality published evidence or historical reluctance to publish negative findings from a clinical trial. Other types of bias derive from human nature. For example, developers can have financial or other stakes in a guideline's recommendations, or they might have preexisting opinions that influence their approach to the literature.

Guideline experts, therefore, have specified desirable guideline qualities and developed criteria for critically appraising guidelines. A 1990 IOM report on guidelines identified credibility and accountability as critical elements (Field and Lohr, 1990). One appraisal tool, the AGREE instrument, defines guideline quality as "the confidence that the potential biases inherent in guideline development have been addressed adequately and that the recommendations are both internally and externally valid, and are feasible for practice" (AGREE Collaboration, 2001). The IOM report, the AGREE instrument, and another widely accepted assessment tool (Shaneyfelt, Mayo-Smith, and Rothwangl, 1999) discuss similar dimensions of guideline quality, including having a well-defined scope and purpose, adequate stakeholder involvement, rigorous and transparent development methods, clear recommendations and presentation, thoroughly considered implementation issues, and editorial independence. Specific criteria in the AGREE instrument are discussed in Chapter Five.

In summary, medical treatment guidelines are systematic statements that assist practitioner, patient, and, in some cases, payor decisions about appropriate health care for specific clinical circumstances. Focusing on defined clinical conditions or populations, guidelines provide recommendations that address specific clinical questions. Guidelines make the most credible, objective recommendations when they are explicitly derived from high-quality evidence, when they are developed with input from relevant stakeholders and specialists, when they address the implications of their recommendations, and when developers cannot be influenced by the funding organization. For the California workers' compensation system, medical treatment guidelines can facilitate decisionmaking regarding appropriateness of care, but they must be credible and objective to do so in a scientific, evidence-based fashion.

Utilization Management

Utilization management (UM) comprises a range of techniques performed by or on behalf of third-party payors to reduce health care costs by assessing the appropriateness or necessity of care provided to individual patients. Specialized medical treatment guidelines, called review criteria, facilitate these coverage decisions. UM is often used to reduce costs by either preventing inappropriate care from being provided or refusing to pay for such care after the fact (Gray and Field, 1989; Wickizer and Lessler, 2002).

UM came into widespread use during the 1980s as public and private third-party payors sought to contain rapidly rising health care costs (Wickizer, 1990;

Ermann, 1988). Earlier, UM had been performed on a retrospective basis by professional standards review organizations (PSROs) in an effort to control hospital utilization for the Medicare program (Wickizer, 1990). This form of UM appeared to have little effect and was abandoned in favor of prospective review. Prospective UM was initially used to authorize hospital inpatient treatment but was later broadened to include review of outpatient surgical procedures and costly diagnostic tests, such as magnetic resonance imaging (MRI).

Studies conducted to date have produced consistent evidence that UM does contain health care costs by reducing utilization. One of the more rigorous early studies of a UM program used by a large private health care insurance carrier showed that UM reduced hospital admissions by about 12 percent, leading to a reduction in total medical expenditures of about 6 percent (Feldstein, Wickizer, and Wheeler, 1988; Wickizer, Wheeler, and Feldstein, 1989). But the effect of UM was found to be much greater for insured groups having *very high* inpatient utilization rates (Feldstein, Wickizer, and Wheeler, 1988). For these groups, UM reduced hospital expenditures by 30 percent. Subsequent research on UM programs used by Blue Cross plans and other large private health insurance carriers showed that UM reduced inpatient expenditures by approximately 10 percent (Khandker and Manning, 1992; Scheffler, Sullivan, and Ko, 1991).

Although UM has been widely used within workers' compensation programs, little research has been conducted to document its effect. One recent study reported data from a case series of approximately 9,500 workers' compensation claimants who were insured by a private insurance carrier and whose medical treatment was subject to review under UM (Wickizer, Lessler, and Franklin, 1999). The total cost savings resulting from denial of medical care deemed to be inappropriate or unnecessary was approximately $5 million.

An ongoing study of UM used by the Washington state workers' compensation program also suggests that UM may be effective in identifying inappropriate or unnecessary medical care (Wickizer et al., 2004). This UM program uses review criteria based on medical treatment guidelines that were developed by the Washington State Department of Labor and Industries in collaboration with the state medical association. Between 1994 and 1998, the medical care of approximately 50,000 workers' compensation claimants was prospectively reviewed, using explicit criteria derived from the guidelines. Denial rates were highest for lumbar fusion (19 percent) and thoracic outlet surgery (20 percent). The most common request reviewed under the guidelines was for lumbar MRI (n = 19,000). Almost one of every ten requests for this imaging procedure was denied. Cost savings from this program have not yet been estimated, but given the denial rates reported (Wickizer et al., 2004), it is certain the UM program will show substantial cost savings.

Research to date indicates that UM can be particularly effective in identifying inappropriate or clinically unnecessary medical care when utilization rates are high

(Feldstein, 1988; Wickizer, 1995), as they are in California workers' compensation. The ultimate success in promoting appropriate use of medical care through UM depends on how well the UM processes are implemented and accepted by the practitioner community.

The UR process, a common element of UM, involves a two-stage assessment of high-cost procedures or services proposed by treating clinicians. Types of care most frequently subject to UR are hospital admissions, prolongation of hospital stay, costly outpatient diagnostic tests, and elective surgical procedures (Wickizer and Lessler, 2002). During the first stage, UR nurses or other staff evaluate proposed care against the review criteria. If the criteria are met, the services are provided. If not, UR physicians may discuss the plans with the patients' treating clinicians and then reassess appropriateness, incorporating both the review criteria and the UR physicians' own clinical judgment. Denials are usually issued by a UR physician rather than a nurse (Gray and Field, 1989; Schlesinger, Gray, and Perriera, 1997).

While this is one typical approach to UR (Wickizer and Lessler, 2002), practices differ substantially across UM organizations. Nationwide, UM organizations exhibit wide variability in other practices as well, particularly in denial-decision appeals. When clinicians request a higher-level review of an initial denial decision, about 15 percent of UM organizations grant an exception more than half of the time, but about 30 percent of UM organizations grant an exception no more than 2 percent of the time (Schlesinger, Gray, and Perriera, 1997).

Although UM decisions hinge on review criteria that identify inappropriate and unnecessary care, there appear to be no clear and widely accepted definitions of *inappropriate care* or *unnecessary care* at this time. In some of the literature, the terms are used interchangeably, while in others, they have distinct meanings. According to one author, these terms represent care that has no significant clinical benefit or care that could be provided in a more cost-effective setting (Wickizer and Lessler, 2002). UM organizations can develop review criteria themselves or purchase proprietary criteria, such as a UM guideline developed by another vendor (Gray and Field, 1989). In about two-thirds of UM organizations, the methods for developing review criteria are formal, systematic, and evidence-based; in the rest, they are less so (Schlesinger, Gray, and Perriera, 1997).

The fact that UR criteria are not always rigorously developed or evidence-based has important implications. UM organizations may have financial incentives to restrict medical care, which creates a potential source of bias in the development and application of the review criteria. The possibility of such bias, by itself, may reduce the credibility of utilization decisions among clinicians and patients. To the degree that bias does affect review criteria development and application, UM can impede the practice of evidence-based medicine. This implies that patients may have inconsistent access to appropriate and necessary medical care, depending on the policies of the UM organization overseeing their care.

In summary, UM represents a range of techniques used to manage health care costs by assessing the appropriateness or necessity of care provided to individual patients. Evidence demonstrates that UM does contain health care costs by reducing utilization, including utilization in workers' compensation systems, although fewer studies have examined UM within those systems than within private health insurance systems. UR is one common technique used by UM organizations to compare care against defined review criteria derived from internally or externally developed guidelines. Nationwide, there appears to be substantial variability in UR criteria and denial-decision appeals, among other practices. This lack of standardization may affect access to and quality of care for patients. In the California workers' compensations system, UM organizations are now required to use review criteria that are in harmony with the utilization schedule or guideline adopted by the state; this may make decisions about appropriate care more consistent across the various UM organizations. In Chapter Eight, we highlight key implementation issues related to the establishment of a UM system for the California workers' compensation system.

CHAPTER THREE

Identifying Guidelines for Work-Related Injury

The first step in our research process was to identify all guidelines that are potentially relevant to work-related injuries, especially musculoskeletal injury guidelines. We did not distinguish between acute and chronic injuries in our search. We used the IOM definition of *guideline*—"systematically developed statements to assist practitioner and patient decisions about appropriate health care for specific clinical circumstances" (Field and Lohr, 1990)—except that we also included documents developed to assist payor decisions, since the legislation called for guidelines addressing utilization issues.

Methods

We employed a number of sources in our search for potentially relevant guidelines:

1. **MEDLINE.** We conducted literature searches in the National Library of Medicine's MEDLINE, using keywords relating to work-related injuries (upper extremity, upper extremity injury, lower extremity, lower extremity injury, spine, spinal injury, back injury, workers compensation). We limited our search to articles published in the three years preceding June 2004 that were designated "practice guidelines."
2. **National Guideline Clearinghouse.** Using keywords and time criteria similar to those used in the MEDLINE search, we searched the National Guideline Clearinghouse website, downloading appropriate guidelines when available or reviewing posted summaries.
3. **State governments.** We contacted each of the other 49 U.S. states to inquire about workers' compensation guidelines. When possible, we downloaded guidelines from state websites. When this was not possible, we wrote to relevant state agencies, requesting the material.
4. **Professional societies.** We searched for guidelines from professional societies, medical organizations, and medical associations. We created a list of potentially relevant organizations, using information from the American Medical Association

(AMA) website, and we then checked each organization's website for relevant guidelines.

5. **Internet searches.** We searched for chiropractic guidelines, physical therapy guidelines, and specialty society websites, using the Google search engine.

6. **Experts.** We asked experts in the field, including providers, insurers, DWC, researchers, and our clinical panelists to identify guidelines relevant to workers' compensation.

7. **Public posting.** We posted a call for guidelines on the DWC website and received a few submissions.

Next, we excluded guidelines that were not in English, not published within the United States, not applicable to adults, or clearly not relevant to work-related injury (e.g., obstetric or cancer-related guidelines). We did not specifically search for acute or chronic injuries, as both types were included in our survey.

Findings

The search identified a large number of guidelines, but many of them overlapped (e.g., guidelines recommended by experts were also found in the National Guideline Clearinghouse search). After we excluded duplicates, we had 72 guidelines to evaluate. These guidelines are listed in Appendix A.

CHAPTER FOUR

Selecting Guidelines for Further Evaluation

The second step in our research process was to narrow our sample of guidelines to those that met the screening criteria listed in Table 4.1. These guidelines met the California Labor Code criteria and had characteristics supported by guideline evaluation literature or desired by CHSWC and DWC.

Methods

Defining Selection Criteria Based on the Legislation

California Labor Code §5307.27 specifies that the medical treatment utilization schedule "shall incorporate . . . evidence-based, peer-reviewed, nationally recognized standards of care" (California Labor Code, 2004). We developed generous definitions for these requirements in order to be inclusive at this stage.

Evidence-Based, Peer-Reviewed. Together, *evidence-based* and *peer-reviewed* were taken to mean based, at a minimum, on a systematic review of literature published in medical journals included in MEDLINE. Systematic reviews of the literature are standard and essential features of an evidence-based guideline development process, as reflected by the fact that they are required by the National Guidelines Clearinghouse and are included in various guideline-assessment methodologies (AGREE Collaboration, 2001; National Guideline Clearinghouse, 2004; Shaneyfelt, Mayo-Smith, and Rothwangl, 1999).

Table 4.1
Screening Criteria for Guidelines Warranting Further Evaluation

Evidence-based, peer-reviewed
Nationally recognized
Address common and costly tests and therapies for injuries of spine, arm, and leg
Reviewed or updated at least every three years
Developed by a multidisciplinary clinical team
Cost less than $500 per individual user in California

Nationally Recognized. *Nationally recognized* was taken to mean any of the following: accepted by the National Guideline Clearinghouse; published in a peer-reviewed U.S. medical journal; developed, endorsed, or disseminated by an organization based in two or more U.S. states; currently used by one or more U.S. state governments; or in wide use in two or more U.S. states.

Developing Selection Criteria with CHSWC and DWC

In conjunction with CHSWC and DWC, we incorporated several additional screening criteria addressing guideline content, quality, and cost. Some of these requirements were based on published literature addressing guideline quality, while other requirements were policy decisions. Some of the potential advantages and disadvantages of these requirements are discussed below.

Address the Most-Common and Costly Tests and Therapies for Spine, Arm, and Leg Injuries. The California Labor Code requires the adopted utilization schedule to address "all treatment procedures and modalities commonly performed in workers' compensation cases." Workers experience a broad range of injuries of the muscles, bones, and joints, as well as other medical problems. These often lead to diagnostic tests, such as X-rays and MRI. In California, common therapies include medication, physical therapy, chiropractic manipulation, joint and soft-tissue injections, and surgical procedures.

Our study considered diagnostic tests and therapies that are not only common, but also costly, either individually or in the aggregate, since UM is a more cost-effective activity when it focuses on such services. For example, Wickizer and colleagues in their workers' compensation UR found that denial of carpal tunnel surgery, arthoscopy, and knee surgery—three common and relatively costly procedures— accounted for the greatest proportion of savings in outpatient treatments. Savings in inpatient treatment were greatest for spinal surgery, a costly and relatively frequently performed surgery in workers' compensation patient populations (Wickizer, Lessler, and Franklin, 1999).

Drawing from a listing of the top 150 procedure codes paid under the Official Medical Fee Schedule (OMFS) for professional and other nonhospital services between January 1, 2000, and June 2002 that was developed by the California Workers' Compensation Institute (CWCI, 2003), we identified the following common tests and therapies that contribute substantially to costs in California:

- MRI of the spine
- Spinal injections
- Spinal surgeries
- Physical therapy
- Chiropractic manipulation
- Surgery for carpal tunnel and other nerve compression syndromes

- Shoulder surgery
- Knee surgery

We considered these cost-driver categories to be the priority topic areas that the state's utilization guideline must cover. Together, they account for about 44 percent of payments under the OMFS for professional and nonhospital services (before consideration of related anesthesia and ancillary services). In addition, using data from an earlier RAND report (Wynn, 2003), we estimated that the surgical procedures account for about 40 percent of payments under the OMFS for inpatient hospital services.

To address the cost-driver topics, the state could (1) choose to have a universe of multiple acceptable guidelines addressing each topic; (2) choose the single best guideline for each topic, putting multiple guidelines together into a patchwork; or (3) choose one guideline set that addresses most or all of them.

The advantages and disadvantages of these alternatives must be compared. A universe of multiple guidelines would create the most flexible decisionmaking for clinicians. However, it might be difficult to implement because each guideline addressing a particular priority topic area could make different recommendations and be of different quality. One objective of having "presumptively correct" guidelines under the law is to improve consistency by making decisionmaking more evidence-based. Having multiple "presumptively correct" guidelines under the law could create confusion in the system and could lead to highly variable decisions by clinicians, claims administrators, medical reviewers, judges, and others.

Using a patchwork of guidelines would enable to state to choose the single highest-quality guideline for each priority topic area, but this approach has disadvantages as well. The different guidelines may vary in rigor of development and frequency of updating. And although each may be selected to address just one priority topic area, the content of two selected guidelines may overlap. For example, one guideline might focus on physical therapy for spinal injuries, and another might focus on surgery for spinal injuries; however, the latter guideline would also be likely to discuss physical therapy before and after surgery. If two guidelines make contradictory recommendations, this could foster appeals and litigation. The adoption of several "presumptively correct" guidelines would be particularly problematic for patients having multiple injuries at the same time, because this would require the use of multiple guidelines. Finally, a patchwork of guidelines may be complex to implement and administer, because the state would have to ensure that all the guidelines are of adequate quality, are updated regularly, and are available to potential users. The costs to users will be greater if the users must purchase multiple proprietary guidelines.

While the use of multiple guideline sets appears to have potential disadvantages for implementation, some of the same problems could affect comprehensive guideline sets as well. Guideline sets may be internally inconsistent on a particular topic, or the sections within each set may be of variable quality. Adopting one set in its entirety implies accepting both stronger and weaker sections.

In hopes of identifying a single guideline set that would address many common and costly work-related injuries in a rigorous, evidence-based fashion, as well as facilitate implementation, we decided to pursue the guideline-set approach at this point in time. The short timeline on this project precluded pursuing this approach and the patchwork approach simultaneously. If we could not identify any acceptable guideline sets, the state would have the option of considering alternative strategies in the future. If existing guideline sets address the cost-driver topic areas in a highly variable or unacceptable fashion, the state can consider compiling a patchwork of guidelines or developing a utilization schedule *de novo*. Thus, for this study, we selected comprehensive guideline sets that address most of the cost-driver tests and therapies to at least some degree.

Reviewed or Updated at Least Every Three Years. To remain evidence-based, guidelines must be updated periodically; therefore, we believe that being current (i.e., developed, updated, or reviewed during the previous three years) and being kept up to date in the future (i.e., having planned future updates or reviews at least every three years) are essential features. The advantage of selecting guidelines that are updated frequently is that clinicians and payors can make decisions based on the current standard of care. This may decrease litigation resulting from the use of guidelines that are out of date relative to published, high-quality evidence. The disadvantage is that this requirement is a relatively high standard. Reviewing and updating are costly activities for developers. Also, the state will have to oversee the process, including ensuring that updates are appropriate for California workers, and this creates administrative costs.

The requirement that the guidelines be reviewed or updated at least every three years was based on prior RAND research. New evidence makes about half of the guidelines out of date after about 5.8 years and at least 10 percent out of date after 3.6 years. The RAND researchers concluded that guidelines should be at least reviewed for potential updating every three years (Shekelle et al., 2001).

Developed by a Multidisciplinary Clinical Team. For many reasons, explained below, RAND recommended that a multidisciplinary clinical team be involved in developing the guidelines. A 1990 IOM report on clinical practice guidelines considered a multidisciplinary development process to be important for guideline quality. The report asserted that a multidisciplinary team increases the likelihood (1) that all relevant scientific evidence will be identified and evaluated, (2) that practical problems in using the guidelines will be identified and addressed, and (3) that affected [provider] groups will see the guidelines as credible and will cooperate in implementing them (Field and Lohr, 1990).

Accepted guideline-assessment tools share the requirement for a multidisciplinary development process (AGREE Collaboration, 2001; Shaneyfelt, Mayo-Smith, and Rothwangl, 1999). The AGREE instrument, for example, asserts that a quality guideline is one that adequately addresses "the potential biases inherent in guideline development." Because providers may consciously or unconsciously bring their own clinical opinions and financial interests to the table when summarizing evidence and formulating guidelines, the AGREE instrument includes the criterion, "the guideline development group includes individuals from all the relevant professional groups" (AGREE Collaboration, 2001). The requirement for a multidisciplinary development team is further supported by earlier RAND/UCLA appropriateness research, which determined that "the composition of a panel clearly influences the ratings [of appropriateness] and those who use a given procedure in practice . . . are more likely to rate it as appropriate than those who do not use the procedure" (Coulter, Adams, and Shekelle, 1995).

Thus, multidisciplinary development teams improve guideline quality and implementation for many reasons. We also believe that a comprehensive guideline set addressing the cost-driver topics—from MRI to injections, surgery, physical therapy, and chiropractic manipulation—should have some input from the specialists rendering these services. The disadvantage of this requirement is that single-specialty panels develop many specialty society guidelines, which means that the requirement could eliminate many of the 72 guidelines we initially identified.

Cost Less Than $500 per Individual User in California. In California, potential users of the medical treatment schedule include insurers and their claims managers, self-insured employers, providers treating injured workers, attorneys, judges, and many other individual users. Some proprietary guidelines addressing work-related injuries are likely to be marketed predominantly to institutional users, such as insurers. We selected a threshold of $500 to eliminate guidelines marketed to institutional rather than individual users.

Applying the Selection Criteria

We were able to determine which guidelines passed some screening criteria, using readily available information. For other criteria, we needed to contact the guideline developers. We therefore applied the criteria in three phases, and we did not obtain information for subsequent phases when a guideline did not meet earlier criteria. The first phase required guidelines to be current (developed or at least reviewed during the past three years), to be nationally recognized, and to address at least two different types of tests and therapies for injuries of the spine, arm, and leg. The second phase required the guidelines to be evidence-based and peer-reviewed, to be developed by a multidisciplinary panel, to be kept up-to-date in the future, and to be available for less than about $500 per individual user in California. These first- and second-phase criteria were publicly posted on the Department of Industrial Relations website in July 2004; the posted document is reproduced in Appendix B. In the third phase, we determined whether the guidelines addressed most of the cost-driver topics discussed above.

We used information obtained during the search process to determine whether a guideline was nationally recognized. We judged whether a guideline was current from dates provided in its content or introductory materials. We determined whether a guideline addressed at least two different types of tests and therapies for injuries of the spine, arm, and leg by examining its content. In making comprehensiveness decisions, we included only sections of each guideline that were reviewed or updated during the past three years.

To determine which guidelines passed the second-phase criteria, we used information included in the guideline content and introductory materials and also contacted the guideline developers for details and corroborating evidence. To verify that systematic literature reviews were performed during the development process, we asked the developers to describe the process and provide us with search terms, databases searched, and other corroborating materials. To verify that there was a multidisciplinary development process, we asked the developers to provide us with materials convincingly demonstrating that at least three different types of specialists treating injured workers were involved. To be considered up-to-date in the future, guideline developers had to document their intention to at least review a guideline every three years. We allowed developers to modify their plans to meet this requirement, if necessary. To meet the cost criterion, developers had to document their intention to make the guideline available to Californians at $500 or less per individual user.

We asked for the required information to be provided to us by August 9, 2004, so that we would have enough time to perform our extensive evaluations. We did, however, make an exception for the American Academy of Orthopedic Surgery (AAOS) guideline, because we did not determine that it was likely to meet our criteria until after August 9.

Finally, we determined whether the guidelines addressed most of our cost-driver topics: MRI of the spine, spinal injections, spinal surgery, physical therapy, chiropractic manipulation, surgery for carpal tunnel and related conditions, shoulder surgery, and knee surgery.

Findings

During the first phase, many guidelines were eliminated because they did not address at least two tests and therapies for injuries of the spine, arm, and leg. A few specialty society documents were excluded because they did not meet our definition of a guideline. Six state guidelines would have passed the first phase of screening if more of their content had been up-to-date. To determine whether this out-of-date content was going to be reviewed in the future, we requested information from the states regarding their plan for updating. All six states gave insufficient information to assure us that their guidelines would be updated according to the required schedule, so we eliminated them from consideration. A few specialty society guidelines were eliminated because we could not confirm an updating plan.

No guidelines were eliminated for lack of a systematic literature review or lack of a multidisciplinary panel, or on the basis of cost. During the third phase, several guidelines were eliminated because they did not address most of the cost drivers to at least a minimal degree.

After we applied all these screening criteria, five comprehensive guideline sets remained eligible for further evaluation. These are listed in Table 4.2.

Table 4.2
Guidelines That Passed All Screening Criteria

Guideline Name	Abbreviated Name	Developer	Year of Last Review
Clinical Guidelines by the American Academy of Orthopedic Surgeons	AAOS	American Academy of Orthopedic Surgeons	2001–2002
American College of Occupational and Environmental Medicine Occupational Medicine Practice Guidelines	ACOEM	American College of Occupational and Environmental Medicine	2003
Optimal Treatment Guidelines, part of Intracorp Clinical Guidelines Tool®	Intracorp	Intracorp	2004
McKesson/InterQual Care Management Criteria and Clinical Evidence Summary	McKesson	McKesson Corporation	2004
Official Disability Guidelines (ODG) – Treatment in Workers' Comp	ODG	Work Loss Data Institute	2004

CHAPTER FIVE

Evaluating the Technical Quality of the Selected Guidelines

The third step in our research process was to evaluate the technical quality of the five selected guidelines. This process entailed two components:

1. Using a standardized method to assess technical quality, including rigor of development, for each guideline.
2. Convening an expert clinical panel to assess how well each guideline addresses utilization issues, including appropriateness and quantity of therapy.

This chapter discusses the first of these evaluations. Guidelines that performed especially poorly on technical quality were to be eliminated from further evaluation.

Methods

Despite the existence of formal, accepted methods for developing guidelines, there is tremendous variation in the rigor of this process (Shaneyfelt, Mayo-Smith, and Rothwangl, 1999). Consequently, an increasing quantity of work has been published on how to critically appraise guidelines after they have been developed. The two appraisal instruments that appear to be most widely accepted are the Shaneyfelt and the AGREE instruments (Hasenfeld and Shekelle, 2003). Both instruments share many similar concepts or evaluation domains but we chose the AGREE instrument for our study because it has been developed and tested internationally and because it has been endorsed by the World Health Organization and is becoming an accepted standard in guidelines development (Grol, Cluzeau, and Burgers, 2003). The supporting material for the AGREE instrument application is also accessible and easy to use.

The AGREE instrument defines the quality of a guideline as "the confidence that the potential biases inherent in guideline development have been addressed adequately and that the recommendations are both internally and externally valid, and are feasible for practice." Using this instrument, we evaluated the five domains listed in Table 5.1: scope and purpose, stakeholder involvement, rigor of development,

Table 5.1
AGREE Instrument Domains and Questions

Scope and purpose:
- The overall objective is specifically described.
- The clinical questions covered by the guidelines are specifically described.
- The patients to whom the guideline is meant to apply are specifically described.

Stakeholder involvement:
- The guideline development group includes individuals from all the relevant professional groups.
- The patients' views and preferences have been sought.
- The target users of the guidelines are clearly defined.
- The guideline has been piloted among target users.

Rigor of development:
- Systematic methods were used to search for evidence.
- The criteria for selecting the evidence are clearly described.
- The methods used for formulating the recommendations are clearly described.
- The health benefits, side effects, and risks have been considered in formulating the recommendations.
- There is an explicit link between the recommendations and the supporting evidence.
- The guideline has been externally reviewed by experts prior to its publication.
- A procedure for updating the guideline is provided.

Clarity and presentation:
- The recommendations are specific and unambiguous.
- The different options for management of conditions are clearly presented.
- Key recommendations are easily identifiable.
- The guideline is supported with tools for application.

Applicability:
- The potential organizational barriers to applying the recommendations have been discussed.
- The potential cost implications of applying the recommendations have been considered.
- Key review criteria are included for monitoring and review purposes.

Editorial independence:
- The guideline is editorially independent from the funding body.
- Conflicts of interest of guideline development members have been recorded.

clarity and presentation, applicability, and editorial independence. More details of the definition of these domains can be found on the AGREE Collaboration's website (AGREE Collaboration, 2001).

To address these domains and their associated questions for the five selected guidelines, we relied upon four sources of information: content of the guidelines themselves, detailed answers to the AGREE instrument questions provided by the guideline developers, telephone interviews with the guideline developers, and corroborating evidence supplied by the developers. All five guideline developers provided detailed answers to the questions, in some cases providing much more relevant information than is found in the guidelines themselves. We also received corroborating evidence convincingly demonstrating that the developers performed systematic searches of the literature, had criteria for selecting evidence and formulating recommendations, convened multidisciplinary panels, and had an updating plan.

Two appraisers, both RAND researchers, reviewed the guidelines. Both researchers have backgrounds in health services research. One is a physician with a Ph.D. in health services, and the other has worked on evidence-based medicine issues at RAND for several years and recently published a study that examines the technical quality of guidelines, using the modified Shaneyfelt instrument (Hasenfeld and Shekelle, 2003). The two appraisers independently reviewed each eligible guideline, the associated explanations, and the corroborating materials. They then rated each question on a scale of 1 to 4. After all eligible guidelines had been assessed, the scores were compiled into overall AGREE standardized domain scores as described in the AGREE instrument. This method adjusts the domain scores for the maximum and minimum possible scores, given the number of questions within a domain and the number of appraisers. Figure 5.1 presents an example of how the standardized domain score was calculated.

The AGREE Collaborative does not recommend basing decisions on an overall guideline score, because domains may not have the same importance in all situations (AGREE Collaboration, 2001). Rigor of development, stakeholder involvement, and editorial independence could be considered the most important domains for this project.

Figure 5.1
Example of Calculating an AGREE Standardized Domain Score

If two appraisers give the following scores for Domain 1 (scope and purpose):

	Item 1	Item 2	Item 3	Total
Appraiser 1	2	3	3	8
Appraiser 2	3	3	4	10
Total	5	6	7	18

Maximum possible score = 4 (strongly agree) x 3 (items) x 2 (appraisers) = 24
Minimum possible score = 1 (strongly disagree) x 3 (items) x 2 (appraisers) = 6

The standardized domain score will be:

$$\frac{(\text{obtained score} - \text{minimum possible score})}{(\text{maximum possible score} - \text{minimum possible score})} =$$

$$\frac{(18 - 6)}{(24 - 6)} = \frac{12}{18} = 0.66$$

Findings

The standardized domain scores for each guideline and domain are shown in Table 5.2. The minimum possible score is 0, and the maximum is 1.0.

Scope and Purpose
Each guideline had a well-described objective, clearly articulated clinical questions, and a defined target population.

Stakeholder Involvement
While each guideline included most relevant professional groups in the guideline development process, patient involvement in the process was not clearly described. A few guidelines were not pilot-tested with target users.

Rigor of Development
All five guidelines scored high in this domain. Each developer clearly described the methods used to search for evidence and formulate recommendations. Updating plans were also provided. However, the developers did not consistently discuss the health benefits and risks of their recommendations or how external experts reviewed their guidelines.

Clarity and Presentation
The RAND researchers found that the recommendations in most of the guidelines were presented clearly and unambiguously.

Applicability
Applying guideline recommendations may require changes in the organization of care, such as establishing a multidisciplinary team to manage specific work-related conditions; in addition, in some circumstances, additional resources may be required

Table 5.2
Technical Quality Evaluation—AGREE Instrument Results
(Standardized Domain Scores)

Domain	AAOS	ACOEM	Intracorp	McKesson	ODG
Scope and purpose	1.00	0.89	0.89	1.00	1.00
Stakeholder involvement	0.54	0.79	0.79	0.88	0.79
Rigor of development	0.81	0.88	0.83	0.88	0.81
Clarity and presentation	0.96	0.88	1.00	1.00	0.96
Applicability	0.17	0.33	0.33	0.61	0.72
Editorial independence	1.00	1.00	0.75	1.00	0.92

to apply recommendations effectively. The developers we contacted tended to make general comments about potential organizational barriers to applying recommendations and cost implications, but few details were discussed. Monitoring and auditing adherence to guideline recommendations can enhance their use. This requires clearly defined review criteria that are derived from the major recommendations themselves (AGREE Collaboration, 2001). Some guidelines did not describe such criteria.

Editorial Independence

All five guideline sets demonstrated the editorial independence of their development group. A few did not discuss potential conflicts of interest of the development members in detail.

Analysis

Scores of the guidelines in this study varied for the different domains. This is consistent with published studies of guideline evaluations from various disciplines. For example, Burgers et al. studied 100 guidelines from 13 countries and found that scores for the different domains varied considerably: scope and purpose, 0.14 to 0.97; stakeholder involvement, 0.06 to 0.60; rigor of development, 0.05 to 0.92; clarity of presentation, 0.11 to 0.88; applicability, 0 to 0.77; editorial independence, 0 to 1.0 (Burgers et al., 2004). Another study of 51 lung-cancer guidelines also demonstrated a wide variation in scores (Harpole et al., 2003). Moreover, as in other studies, our selected guidelines scored less well in the stakeholder involvement and applicability domains. In contrast, our guidelines scored higher in rigor of development and editorial independence. Overall, the scores of our five study guidelines were higher than those reported in the two studies cited above. Even though we feel that stakeholder involvement, rigor of development, and editorial independence are the most important domains in the technical evaluation, the low scores in the applicability domain should not be ignored, as they may indicate that guideline developers are not giving adequate consideration to issues pertinent to guideline implementation.

Nevertheless, we felt that since all five of our study guidelines did fairly well in the technical quality evaluation, none warranted elimination on this basis. This process ensured that the guidelines we presented our clinical panelists were developed according to rigorous methods and were relatively free of bias.

The low applicability scores of three guidelines warrant some further discussion, however. While our clinical panelists did not consider applicability, our stakeholder interviews addressed the application of the ACOEM guideline for UM purposes during the year or so preceding the study. The stakeholder panel meeting also considered the application of medical treatment guidelines for utilization decisions. These issues are discussed further in Chapter Seven.

CHAPTER SIX

Evaluating the Clinical Content of the Selected Guidelines

The second step in our detailed evaluation was the convening of a multidisciplinary panel of expert clinicians to evaluate the content of our five selected guidelines. Our objective was to determine how well each guideline addresses appropriateness and quantity of treatment, particularly for the cost-driver topics discussed previously.

We asked the panelists to evaluate in somewhat greater detail ten subtopics selected from the cost-driver topics. In addition, we asked them to consider the overall content of each guideline and also to rate and rank the guidelines as a whole. We selected panelists representing a diversity of specialties, locations, and clinical-practice settings. It is important to note that we were attempting to accomplish this evaluation within a limited project scope and time frame. Because of these constraints, we were unable to undertake any independent literature review or guideline development. Therefore, unlike our evaluation of technical quality, our conclusions about the guideline content are only as valid as the judgments of our expert clinicians.

Methods

Adapting an Evaluation Method from the RAND/UCLA Appropriateness Method

To our knowledge, there are no established methods for evaluating or comparing the clinical content of guidelines; therefore, we developed an evaluation method by adapting parts of the RAND/UCLA Appropriateness Method (RAM). RAM is an expert-clinical-panel method designed to facilitate the measurement of overuse and underuse of medical and surgical procedures. It produces a set of criteria for determining the appropriateness of a particular procedure under a variety of clinical circumstances (Fitch et al., 2001).

We used RAM as our framework for several reasons. Importantly, its purpose is consistent with a principal objective of our study, i.e., to evaluate how well existing guidelines address the appropriateness of selected procedures under a variety of clinical circumstances. Further, RAM is a rigorous method for integrating expert opinion and available evidence, extending judgment into areas where the evidence is unclear. By allowing for discussion, it uses an iterative approach to formulating recommendations. It forces panelists to consider component parts in making summative judgments. In contrast to consensus-based-panel methods, it does not force consensus where none is forthcoming. As noted in Chapter Two, RAM has been used extensively over the past 20 years. When used for its original purpose, it has produced moderately consistent (i.e., reliable) recommendations and has had predictive validity (Shekelle 2004; Shekelle et. al., 1998; Shekelle, Chassin, and Park, 1998).

When using RAM to develop appropriateness criteria, its intended purpose, the researchers' first step is a detailed literature review synthesizing the latest available scientific evidence on the procedure being evaluated. At the same time, the researchers develop a very detailed list of clinical scenarios under which the procedure may be used; these are called indications. The indications are grouped according to the patients' primary symptoms and reasons for seeking care. The researchers then select a panel of expert clinicians recommended by specialty societies. These clinicians review written synopses of the literature review and apply them to the lists of indications. Using the synthesized literature and their own clinical judgment, the clinicians rate the expected benefit-to-harm ratio of the procedures on a scale from 1 (lowest) to 9 (highest). A rating of 5 means the benefits and harms are equal or that the clinician is unable to make a judgment for that indication.

The clinicians rate the indications twice in a two-round "modified Delphi" process. During the first round, panelists rate the indications individually. In the second round, they meet for one to two days under the guidance of an individual experienced in the RAM method. At this time, each panelist receives a summary of his or her ratings and of the group's ratings. The panelists discuss the ratings, focusing on areas of disagreement. Each panelist then re-rates the benefit-to-harm ratio for each indication. No attempt is made to reach consensus among the panelists; the objective is to determine whether any disagreements are caused by real differences in clinical understanding.

The researchers then analyze the panel ratings to determine whether the procedure is appropriate, uncertain, or inappropriate for each indication. A procedure is inappropriate for a given indication when the median panel rating is 1 to 3 and there is no disagreement among the panelists. A procedure is appropriate for a given indication when the median panel rating is 7 to 9 and there is no disagreement. A median of 4 to 6 or disagreement indicates that appropriateness is uncertain. RAM employs specific definitions of disagreement that are beyond the scope of this discussion; the definitions employed in our study are provided below.

The end result is a list of specific clinical circumstances under which the procedure should not be provided because it is inappropriate; RAM defines performing such procedures as overuse. Another list of clinical circumstances represents appropriate use; failing to provide appropriate care is defined as underuse. In the remaining clinical circumstances, it is unclear whether use would be appropriate or not; performing the procedure under such circumstances constitutes neither overuse nor underuse.

We used many components of RAM to determine how well each of our five selected guidelines addresses appropriateness and quantity of treatment, as described below. A very detailed and rigorous way of adapting RAM for this purpose might include

- Reviewing and synthesizing the clinical literature for each narrowly defined therapy under consideration
- Defining very specific categories of indications for each therapy
- Identifying content within each of the guidelines that addresses each indication
- Having expert clinicians rate the validity of the guideline content addressing each indication

Unfortunately, this approach would be incredibly resource-intensive. It would require detailed literature reviews addressing both the appropriateness and quantity of care for the many topics within each guideline set. Identifying content for narrowly defined therapies and indications would also be very labor-intensive because each guideline set is organized differently. The clinical panel would have to spend many days rating the content during the two rounds. Indeed, we decided that the resources required for this approach could be substantially greater than those required for developing guidelines *de novo*.

To work within our limited time frame, we adapted RAM in a less precise form. We were unable to review the clinical literature, and we did not create detailed lists of indications for narrowly defined therapies but rather consolidated many similar types of therapies together into very broad categories. We did identify content relevant to each broad category, and we asked the panelists to consider whether the content adequately describes detailed indications for clearly defined therapies. Instead of having panelists rate the validity of content for detailed indications, as one might do in an ideal approach, we had them rate guideline validity and comprehensiveness for broad categories.

Developing Evaluation Criteria That Address Utilization Decisions

The California Labor Code stipulates that the utilization schedule "shall address, at a minimum, . . . frequency, duration, intensity, and appropriateness," i.e., the schedule must address utilization decisions. Therefore, in adapting RAM for the purpose of evaluating guidelines, we needed criteria to assess how well the guideline content addresses utilization decisions. First, a guideline must recommend whether or not common therapies should be provided to injured workers in specific clinical circumstances, i.e., whether such care is appropriate to the circumstances. Second, when care can be quantified and can be provided in a variable fashion, guidelines should also outline the quantity of therapy indicated. Guideline content addressing appropriateness and quantity of therapy was therefore the principal focus of the clinical assessment.

We adapted our definition of appropriateness from RAM (Fitch et al., 2001):

> An appropriate procedure [or modality] is one in which the expected health benefit (e.g., improved functional capacity, . . . increased life expectancy) exceeds the expected negative consequences [to the patient] (e.g., mortality, morbidity, . . . time lost from work) by a sufficiently wide margin that the procedure [or modality] is worth doing, exclusive of cost.

To facilitate utilization decisions, guideline recommendations addressing the appropriateness of a particular therapy should be both comprehensive and valid. We decided that

- To comprehensively address appropriateness, a guideline's treatment recommendations should define whether the therapy is appropriate, inappropriate, or uncertain for most patients who might be considered candidates.
- Valid recommendations should be evidence-based or, in the absence of evidence, consistent with expert opinion.

Adapting the RAM method for defining indications, we considered a guideline's content addressing the appropriateness of a therapy to include descriptions of

- The specific clinical circumstances (patient characteristics such as symptoms, medical history, physical findings, and diagnostic test results) under which use would be clearly appropriate.
- The specific clinical circumstances under which use would be clearly inappropriate.
- The clinical circumstances under which use is uncertain; these can be defined by exception, i.e., by the absence of circumstances for which use would be either clearly appropriate or clearly inappropriate.

Quantity of therapy includes three related concepts specified in the legislation: frequency, intensity, and duration. Lacking established definitions for these terms, we defined *frequency* as the number of procedures or modalities provided to a patient in a given time interval. *Intensity* was defined as medication dose or potency, the relative force exerted by or on a patient during physical modalities, and other measures quantifying a variably performed procedure or modality. *Duration* was defined as the time interval over which a given procedure or modality is provided to a patient at a particular frequency or intensity. We decided that

- To be comprehensive in addressing quantity for a particular therapy, a guideline's recommendations should define frequency, intensity, and duration for most of the patients the guideline considers appropriate or uncertain candidates.
- To be valid in addressing the quantity of a particular therapy, a guideline's treatment recommendations should be evidence-based or consistent with expert opinion.

We applied these definitions to the rating process as follows: We asked panelists to review guideline content relating to a particular type of therapy and then to judge whether the content addressing the appropriateness of the therapy was comprehensive and valid. We also asked them to judge whether the content addressing quantity was comprehensive and valid.

Defining and Identifying the Guideline Content to Be Evaluated

The next step in developing our evaluation methods was defining and identifying the guideline content to be evaluated. Given the project's scope and timeline, we could not ask the panelists to evaluate all guideline content in detail. However, we wanted to compare the guidelines on important therapies, as well as overall.

Selected Subtopics. Several tests and therapies that are common and costly in the California workers' compensation system are listed in Chapter Four. For the clinical evaluation, we focused on ten subtopics selected, using the following rationale, from among these cost-driver topic areas.

For a variety of reasons, including constraints of scope and time frame, we were unable to have the panelists evaluate guideline content addressing all of the cost-driver topic areas. Therefore, we selected subtopics on the basis of the following: We wanted to address regions of the body that are frequently injured at work, such the spine, the large proximal joints in the extremities, and more-distal joints in the extremities. For each selected region, we sought a broad range of common and costly tests and therapies, including physical modalities and surgical procedures. In selecting regions of the body and tests or therapies, we preferred situations for which the guidelines had different recommendations. For example, all the guidelines made similar recommendations about MRI of the spine and knee surgery, so comparing them on these topics seemed to offer little benefit. We also ensured that the panel included practitioners providing the services under consideration. For example, because there was no radiologist on the panel, it would have been difficult to evaluate MRI of the spine or spinal injections. Therefore, we eliminated MRI of the spine, knee surgery, and spinal injections.

One of the cost-driver categories included carpal tunnel surgery and other nerve compression syndromes. To simplify the discussion of these conditions, which occur in diverse parts of the body, we decided to focus on the most common one, carpal tunnel syndrome. This narrowed a broad cost-driver category into a single, easily defined diagnosis.

When addressing the physical modalities, we distinguished physical therapy modalities from chiropractic modalities. We defined physical therapy modalities as therapies provided by physical therapists, and chiropractic manipulation as any additional therapies that can be provided only by chiropractors. This meant that for rating purposes, chiropractic care was generally considered synonymous with manipulation. According to the California chiropractors we spoke with, manipulation is performed not only for the spine, but also for the shoulder, elbow, wrist, hip, knee, ankle, and even the smallest extremity joints.

Distinguishing physical therapy modalities from chiropractic ones so sharply is somewhat artificial, but we had both a scientific and a policy-relevant rationale. In practice, there appears to be overlap between the physical modalities provided by chiropractors and those provided by physical therapists. According to many chiropractors with whom we spoke, chiropractors provide some of the same modalities physical therapists do and also manipulate. It was important to distinguish physical therapy modalities from chiropractic ones for our evaluation because we did not want panelists to rate the physical therapy content twice. It was also important to distinguish physical therapy modalities from chiropractic ones for policy reasons, because in California, chiropractors are supposed to provide physical therapy modalities only "in the course of chiropractic manipulations and/or adjustments" (California Laws and Regulations Relating to the Practice of Chiropractic). Thus, the appropriateness of manipulation is critical to determining whether a chiropractor should provide any physical modalities for a particular injury.

In the end, the following ten subtopics were selected:

- Lumbar spine problems
  1. Physical therapy
  2. Chiropractic manipulation
  3. Surgery, decompression procedures (laminectomy and discectomy)
  4. Surgery, fusion procedures (arthrodesis and instrumentation)
- Carpal tunnel syndrome
  5. Physical therapy
  6. Chiropractic manipulation
  7. Surgery
- Shoulder injuries
  8. Physical therapy
  9. Chiropractic manipulation
  10. Surgery

These ten subtopics include two broad categories of injuries (lumbar spine and shoulder) and one discrete diagnosis (carpal tunnel syndrome). One advantage of considering a discrete diagnosis in addition to the broad categories is that it might enable us to see whether lumping many diagnoses together influences the results of the evaluation.

Before the meeting, we provided the panelists with booklets containing the content relevant to these ten selected therapies. A team of clinicians (a registered nurse, a family physician, and an occupational medicine expert) identified content within each guideline that addressed appropriateness and quantity for each topic. This content was compiled by body region and by guideline, and the clinicians annotated the content to identify the therapy type (physical therapy, chiropractic manipulation, or surgery).

Residual Content. Although all five guidelines addressed the selected topics in detail, the residual (i.e., nonselected) content within each guideline varied somewhat in scope. We asked panelists to rate the residual content of each guideline as though it were a separate topic, considering appropriateness and quantity of therapy. We also asked them to focus particularly on therapies that are common and costly in workers' compensation systems. Each panelist was provided with electronic access to the entire content of the five guideline sets, and each rated the comprehensiveness and validity of the residual content.

Entire Content. After rating the selected topics and the residual content, the panelists were asked to rate the entire content of each guideline. The focus remained on appropriateness and quantity for therapies that are common and costly in workers' compensation systems. Panelists evaluated each guideline set, considering whether it was comprehensive, evidence-based, and valid. Although being evidence-based is a component of being valid, we wanted to distinguish guidelines panelists felt were based on evidence from those they felt were based on valid clinical opinions. We wanted to address whether the guidelines were evidence-based because of comments we had heard from some California stakeholders indicating that they did believe the ACOEM guideline set was evidence-based. After rating the entire content, the panelists were asked to rank the guidelines on the same bases they used to rate the entire content.

Selecting Clinical Panelists

The third step in our evaluation process, selecting clinical panelists, was adapted directly from RAM. Our objective was to convene a national panel of experts in musculoskeletal injuries, specifically, clinicians who were actively practicing at least 20 percent of the time and who had some experience treating injured workers. All panelists were referred to us by national specialty societies. Eight societies, representing a broad spectrum of providers caring for injured workers, provided nominations. The only desired specialty that was not represented among our nominees was radiology.

After receiving the nominations, we contacted each nominee to determine his or her interest and potential availability for our panel date. We then requested curriculum vitae. We selected panelists on the basis of the following attributes: national balance (we wanted no more than about 20 percent of the panelists to be from California); diversity of practice setting (academic vs. nonacademic); evidence of leadership in their specialty; diversity of experience treating injured workers (from modest to substantial experience); expertise in evidence-based medicine; experience developing, implementing, or evaluating guidelines; experience with panels; and lack of direct involvement with any of the guidelines under review. We sought to have two panelists experienced in therapies not commonly ordered or provided by other panel members, in order to increase the discussion related to those topics.

The most promising candidates were interviewed by telephone to determine relevant experience, attitude toward the use of evidence-based medicine for UM purposes, potential conflicts of interest, and self-described ability to function within a team. Because this last attribute is so central to the success of expert panels, we also contacted references before offering the nominees positions on the panel.

The final 11-member clinician panel included one general internal medicine physician, two occupational medicine physicians, one physical medicine and rehabilitation physician, one physical therapist, one neurologist also board-certified in pain management, two doctors of chiropractic medicine, two orthopedic surgeons, and one neurosurgeon. The selection methods and the names of the panelists are given in Appendix C.

Two-Round Rating Process

Following the RAM method, panelists rated the guidelines in a two-round process. During the first round, they rated the guidelines individually. In the second round, they met on October 1 and 2, 2004.

Round One. The selected clinical panelists received the round-one materials about three weeks before the panel meeting. These materials included a highly detailed set of instructions and definitions used by the study, booklets containing guideline content for the ten selected subtopics, instructions for accessing electronic versions of the entire guidelines, and rating forms. Sample rating forms for round one are shown in Appendix D. Because we did not determine that the AAOS guideline passed all the screening criteria until a few days after the initial mailing, we sent materials and rating forms for this guideline set separately. RAND staff contacted the panelists by electronic mail and, when necessary, by telephone to clarify questions about the rating process and to facilitate electronic access to the entire content of the five guideline sets.

Panelists rated the comprehensiveness and validity of content addressing the ten selected therapies (considering appropriateness and quantity separately). They then rated the comprehensiveness and validity of the residual content (considering appropriateness and quantity together). For the entire-content evaluation, they considered whether the entire content was comprehensive, evidence-based, and valid (appropriateness and quantity were considered together). Panelists rated each item on a scale of 1 to 9, with 1 being lowest and 9 being highest. A rating of 5 indicated intermediate judgments or total uncertainty. Panelists ranked the guidelines on a scale of 1 to 5.

RAND staff collected and analyzed the individual ratings and distributed them to all the panelists just prior to the second-round face-to-face meeting.

Round Two. As stated in the RAM manual,

> The purpose of the second round is to give the panelists the opportunity to discuss their ratings face to face, in light of their knowledge of how all the other panelists rated. Generally, the panel moderator will focus on [topics] where there is considerable dispersion in the panel ratings to find out if there is genuine clinical disagreement about appropriateness (Fitch et al., 2001).

Unlike the consensus-panel method, the appropriateness method does not force agreement among panelists. The purpose of the discussion is to allow different points of view to be expressed and to contend with one another, bringing each panelist's understanding closer to a true one. Once all points of view have been aired, the chair asks the panelists to re-rate the item in each question, even if agreement has not been reached.

A member of the RAND staff—a practicing rheumatologist experienced in the RAM method—chaired the panel meeting. At the start of the meeting, RAND staff provided panelists with a summary of the technical evaluation results for each guideline. Panelists also received a summary sheet displaying the groups' findings in terms of comprehensiveness and validity for each guideline set and subtopic.

In response to questions that arose during the first-round process, we provided the following rating guidance for the second round:

- If panelists were completely unfamiliar with a topic, they were reminded to select the middle rating, 5.
- If a guideline had no content addressing appropriateness or quantity of therapy, panelists were instructed to select 1 for comprehensiveness and validity (indicating that there was no valid content).
- If a guideline had minimal content addressing appropriateness or quantity of therapy, panelists were instructed to select 2 for comprehensiveness and then assess the validity of the content as usual.
- If a guideline said a therapy should never be used, panelists were instructed to select 9 for comprehensiveness and then assess the validity of the recommendation as usual (i.e., a rating of 9 meant the panelist thought the therapy should never be used).

Second-round rating forms were the same as those for the first round except that they also displayed, next to each question, the relevant results from the first round, including the distribution of ratings, the median, the absolute deviation, and any disagreement. The forms were tailored for each panelist, with a symbol (^) identifying the rating the panelist had selected for each question. The round-one results were formatted in the manner demonstrated in Appendix E.

After discussing the quality of each guideline's content for a particular topic, panelists re-rated each question. Before having panelists rate and rank the entire content of each guideline, we discussed the summary sheets displaying the groups' findings in the first round, particularly any inconsistencies observed in the data.

Analysis. We assessed the panelists' rankings of comprehensiveness, evidence-basis, and validity as follows, where *Yes* means the content is comprehensive, evidence-based, or valid, depending on the question; *No* means the opposite; and *Uncertain* is inconclusive.

- Yes: panel median of 7 to 9, without disagreement
- Uncertain: panel median of 4 to 6, or any median with disagreement
- No: panel median of 1 to 3, without disagreement

Although we used definitions employed by prior RAM studies, we selected a higher bar for disagreement for this study than has been selected for some previous appropriateness panels. Because the members of our panel represented disparate specialties, rated large quantities of content over a limited number of dimensions, and did not have a literature review to support their decisions, we believed that disagreement might result from these factors rather than from real differences over the quality of guideline content. To define disagreement, we started from a standard RAM definition for an 11-member panel: four or more panelists rated in the 1 to 3 range and four or more rated in the 7 to 9 range. We then modified the definition in a manner discussed in the RAM manual: We threw out one high and one low rating. This relaxed the definition of disagreement somewhat, increasing the likelihood that the panel would reach agreement.

For the rankings, we determined the median ranking score for each guideline.

Findings

Ratings

A summary of the panelists' ratings is presented Tables 6.1 through 6.4; the complete ratings are given in Appendix E. Overall, each guideline set had important validity and comprehensiveness limitations.

We found that all five guideline sets addressed the appropriateness of some types of surgery, as shown in Table 6.1. Panelists agreed that the AAOS guideline was valid and comprehensive for lumbar spinal decompression and fusion surgeries. They were uncertain whether it was valid for carpal tunnel surgery and agreed that it was not comprehensive in addressing shoulder surgery. Panelists agreed that the ACOEM guideline was valid and comprehensive for lumbar spinal decompression surgery, carpal tunnel surgery, and shoulder surgery. Validity was uncertain for lumbar spinal fusion surgery. Panelists agreed that the Intracorp guideline was valid and comprehensive for shoulder surgery and invalid for lumbar spinal fusion surgery; the other two topics were of uncertain validity. The McKesson guidelines were given the same ratings for surgical topics as the ACOEM guidelines were. For the ODG guideline, carpal tunnel surgery and shoulder surgery were both rated comprehensive and valid; the other two topics were of uncertain validity.

As seen in Table 6.2, appropriateness of physical modalities is rarely addressed well by the five guideline sets. Panelists were uncertain of the validity of the AAOS guideline for two topics and agreed that it was not comprehensive for the other four. Panelists agreed that the ACOEM guideline was valid and comprehensive for physical therapy of the shoulder. They agreed that it was not comprehensive for chiropractic manipulation of the shoulder. Validity was uncertain for the other four topics. Panelists agreed that the ACOEM guideline was not valid for chiropractic manipulation of the spine and carpal tunnel. Validity was uncertain for the remaining topics. They agreed that the McKesson guideline was valid and comprehensive for chiropractic manipulation of the carpal tunnel and physical therapy of the shoulder and that it was not comprehensive in addressing chiropractic manipulation of the shoulder. Validity was uncertain for the other three topics. Panelists agreed that the

Table 6.1
Panelists' Assessment of the Comprehensiveness and Validity of Content Addressing the Appropriateness of Surgical Procedures

	AAOS	ACOEM	Intracorp	McKesson	ODG
Lumbar spinal decompression	**Yes**	**Yes**	Validity uncertain	**Yes**	Validity uncertain
Lumbar spinal fusion	**Yes**	Validity uncertain	Not valid	Validity uncertain	Validity uncertain
Carpal tunnel surgery	Validity uncertain	**Yes**	Validity uncertain	**Yes**	**Yes**
Shoulder surgery	Not comprehensve	**Yes**	**Yes**	**Yes**	**Yes**

NOTE: *Yes* means the panel agreed that the content was both comprehensive and valid. *Not comprehensive* means the panel agreed that the guideline was not comprehensive; we assume minimal relevant content and do not report validity. *Not valid* means the content was of uncertain or better comprehensiveness and the panel agreed that the content was not valid. *Validity uncertain* means the content was of uncertain or better comprehensiveness and the panelists were uncertain of validity.

Table 6.2
Panelists' Assessment of the Comprehensiveness and Validity of Content Addressing the Appropriateness of Physical Modalities

	AAOS	ACOEM	Intracorp	McKesson	ODG
Lumbar spine physical therapy	Validity uncertain	Validity uncertain	Validity uncertain	Validity uncertain	Validity uncertain
Lumbar spine chiropractic	Not comprehensive	Validity uncertain	Not valid	Validity uncertain	Validity uncertain
Carpal tunnel physical therapy	Not comprehensive	Validity uncertain	Validity uncertain	Validity uncertain	**Yes**
Carpal tunnel chiropractic	Not comprehensive	Validity uncertain	Not valid	**Yes**	**Yes**
Shoulder physical therapy	Validity uncertain	**Yes**	Validity uncertain	**Yes**	Validity uncertain
Shoulder chiropractic	Not comprehensive	Not comprehensive	Validity uncertain	Not comprehensive	Not comprehensive

ODG guideline was valid and comprehensive for physical therapy and chiropractic manipulation of the carpal tunnel and that it was not comprehensive in addressing chiropractic manipulation of the shoulder. Validity was uncertain for the other three topics.

Quantity of physical modalities is rarely addressed well by the five guidelines, as is evident from Table 6.3. Panelists agreed that the AAOS guideline was not comprehensive in addressing the six quantity topics. They agreed that the ACOEM guideline was valid and comprehensive for physical therapy of the carpal tunnel.

Table 6.3
Panelists' Assessment of the Comprehensiveness and Validity of Content Addressing the Quantity of Physical Modalities

	AAOS	ACOEM	Intracorp	McKesson	ODG
Lumbar spine physical therapy	Not comprehensive	Validity uncertain	Validity uncertain	Validity uncertain	Validity uncertain
Lumbar spine chiropractic	Not comprehensive	Not comprehensive	Not valid	Validity uncertain	Validity uncertain
Carpal tunnel physical therapy	Not comprehensive	Not comprehensive	Validity uncertain	Validity uncertain	Validity uncertain
Carpal tunnel chiropractic	Not comprehensive	**Yes**	Not valid	**Yes**	Validity uncertain
Shoulder physical therapy	Not comprehensive	**Valid**, comprehensiveness uncertain	Validity uncertain	Validity uncertain	**Yes**
Shoulder chiropractic	Not comprehensive	Not comprehensive	Validity uncertain	Not comprehensive	Not comprehensive

They also agreed that it was valid for physical therapy of the shoulder but were uncertain of its comprehensiveness. Validity was uncertain for physical therapy of the spine. Panelists agreed it was not comprehensive for the remaining three topics. They agreed that the Intracorp guideline was not valid for chiropractic manipulation of the spine and carpal tunnel and of uncertain validity for all physical therapy topics. Panelists agreed it was not comprehensive for chiropractic manipulation of the shoulder. Panelists agreed that the McKesson guideline was comprehensive and valid for chiropractic manipulation of the carpal tunnel and that it was not comprehensive for chiropractic manipulation of the shoulder. Validity was uncertain for the remaining topics. Panelists agreed that the ODG guideline was comprehensive and valid for physical therapy of the shoulder and that it was not comprehensive for chiropractic manipulation of the shoulder. Validity was uncertain for the remaining topics.

Table 6.4 presents summary results for each guideline, reiterating the appropriateness ratings, then presenting the residual-content and the entire-content evaluations. To summarize, the panelists thought that all five guidelines require substantial improvement, but they preferred ACOEM:

1. The AAOS guideline addressed appropriateness well for two of the four surgical topics and none of the six physical modality topics. Panelists agreed that the guideline had little residual content. In the entire-content rating, they agreed that the guideline was valid and evidence-based but were uncertain whether it was comprehensive. It was ranked last.

Table 6.4
Clinical Evaluation Summary: Panelists' Assessment of Comprehensiveness and Validity

	AAOS	ACOEM	Intracorp	McKesson	ODG
Appropriateness					
Surgery	2 of 4 topics	3 of 4 topics	1 of 4 topics	3 of 4 topics	2 of 4 topics
Physical therapy and chiropractic	0 of 6 topics	1 of 6 topics	0 of 6 topics	2 of 6 topics	2 of 6 topics
Residual Content					
	Not compre-hensive	Validity uncertain	Validity uncertain	Validity uncertain	Validity uncertain
Entire Content					
Rating	**Valid**, compre-hensiveness uncertain	**Valid**, compre-hensiveness uncertain	Not valid	Validity uncertain	Validity uncertain
Median rank	4	**1**	3	2	2

2. The ACOEM guideline addressed appropriateness well for three of the four surgical topics and one of the six physical modalities. Panelists were uncertain whether the residual content was valid. In the entire-content rating, panelists agreed the guideline was valid but were uncertain about whether it was comprehensive or evidence-based. ACOEM was ranked first.

3. The Intracorp guideline addressed appropriateness well for one of the four surgical topics and none of the six physical modalities. Panelists were uncertain whether the residual content was valid. In the entire-content rating, panelists agreed the guideline was not valid or evidence-based. It was ranked third.

4. The McKesson guideline addressed appropriateness well for three of the four surgical topics and two of the six physical modalities. In the residual- and entire-content evaluations, panelists were uncertain about whether it was valid or evidence-based. This guideline tied for second.

5. The ODG guideline addressed appropriateness well for two of the four surgical topics and two of the six physical modalities. In the residual- and entire-content evaluations, panelists were uncertain about whether it was valid or evidence-based. This guideline tied for second.

Panelists' Comments

Panelists' qualitative comments and discussion tone and content during the meeting may be informative for interpreting the results presented above. There were multiple opportunities for comment during the evaluation process. Both the first- and second-round rating forms had room for comments below each question. The second round of ratings involved discussion before each topic was rated for each guideline. Finally, panelists were given the opportunity to comment at the conclusion of the meeting. Concluding comments are given in Appendix F. The following is a summary of key issues raised.

Panelists appeared comfortable rating the surgical topics, based on their personal understanding of the relevant literature. However, panelists providing or ordering physical modalities and those not providing or ordering those services had quite different understandings. Some physicians were relatively unfamiliar with certain physical modalities, such as chiropractic manipulation of the carpal tunnel and shoulder. Providers of such services cited published literature for their specialties, and some physicians admitted being unfamiliar with that literature. For some physical modality topics, there appears to be little literature at this time. For example, the two chiropractors, both experienced in applying evidence-based medicine and developing or using chiropractic guidelines, were aware of only two preliminary studies addressing chiropractic manipulation of the carpal tunnel. Quantity of care also appeared to be relatively unaddressed by the existing literature.

During the concluding remarks, seven of the 11 panelists volunteered that

- The five selected guidelines "are not as valid as everyone would want in a perfect world."
- "They do not meet or exceed standards; they barely meet standards."
- "California could do a lot better by starting from scratch" and developing its own guidelines.

Several panelists reported preferring the clinical guidelines over the proprietary ones marketed for UM purposes, which they found too "proscriptive," meaning that the proprietary guidelines limit clinical options to a degree that made the panelists uncomfortable.

Individual panelists mentioned that all five guidelines are weak in discussing return to work, addressing practice patterns in use (especially for chiropractic manipulation and physical therapy), and specifying which type of surgeon can perform a particular procedure. One panelist remarked that the guidelines could use a scientific editor to make them more readable. Some panelists felt that if guideline development were pursued, the existing guidelines would be a good starting point in the process and input from specialty societies would also be valuable.

Some panelists noted limitations in our guideline-evaluation method. One panelist thought the proprietary guidelines and the clinical guidelines were not comparable, because "some of the guidelines are good for providers to use, others are good for case managers." Another panelist thought that having broad topics such as surgery for shoulder injuries is like asking someone to rate a whole guideline on chest pain—i.e., our unit of analysis was too broad. This individual felt that we should have used the literature to develop specific recommendations for individual patients.

Conclusions from the Guideline Evaluations

The clinical content evaluation leads us to the following conclusions:

- All five guideline sets appear far less than ideal; in the words of the panelists, they barely meet standards.
- The clinical panel preferred the ACOEM guideline set to the alternatives and considered it valid but of uncertain comprehensiveness in the entire-content rating.
- The ACOEM guideline set addresses cost-driver surgical topics well for three of the four therapies the panel rated.
- The ACOEM guideline set does not address lumbar spinal fusion well, but the AAOS guideline set does.

- The ACOEM guideline set does not appear to address physical modalities very well, but the other four sets do little better.
- Panelists were uncertain whether the residual content in the ACOEM guidelines is valid.

Analysis

The panelists' comments may shed light on the reasons for internal inconsistencies in our findings. One notable inconsistency is that the ACOEM and McKesson guidelines were rated similarly for the selected topics and for the residual content, yet the ACOEM was judged valid overall and the McKesson was not. As an analogy, one plus one equaled two for the McKesson guideline set but equaled three for the ACOEM set. When asked about this, some panelists explained that the McKesson guideline was overly proscriptive, as noted above. The underlying reason for this opinion may be that clinicians are biased against guidelines marketed for UM purposes or biased in favor of specialty society guidelines. Alternatively, the McKesson guideline may be overly proscriptive, limiting care options to an unacceptable degree.

Another inconsistency is the fact that all five guidelines did reasonably well in the technical quality evaluation yet were rated only mediocre in the clinical content evaluation, particularly for the physical modalities. It may be that rigorously developed guidelines still use expert opinion to fill gaps in the evidence. Such gaps appear common for physical modality issues, particularly quantity of care and chiropractic manipulation of the wrist. Panelists are less likely to agree that opinion-based recommendations are valid. Also, physicians might not know that chiropractors manipulate the extremities, making it difficult for physicians to develop or assess guidelines for such modalities. Finally, although one would expect good technical quality, including rigorous development methods, to produce valid clinical content, we know of no studies addressing this.

Panelists agreed that the ACOEM guideline set is valid but not that it is evidence-based. This inconsistency suggests that panelists thought the ACOEM is valid but that its recommendations rest on expert opinion. A number of stakeholders also mentioned to us that they did not believe the ACOEM guideline set is evidence-based. Closer examination of the scores (given in Appendix E) suggests that panelists thought the ACOEM is mostly evidence-based: nine of 11 panelists rated the guideline set at 6 or higher on a scale of 1 to 9, with a median rating of 6. Seven panelists rated it 6 or higher on validity, with a median score of 7.

Our methods have important limitations that might also help to explain these inconsistencies. First, we were unable to provide panelists with literature reviews for the therapies under consideration. This is an especially important limitation for the evaluations of the physical modalities because panelists understood this literature differently, and some panelists were not at all familiar with the relevant literature on chiropractic manipulation of the carpal tunnel.

Second, in most RAND/UCLA appropriateness studies, panelists assess appropriateness for well-defined surgeries and categories of patients (Fitch et al., 2001). In contrast, we aggregated large amounts of clinical material and asked panelists to provide summary judgments. This may mean that panelists were averaging highly valid content with invalid content, leading to intermediate, i.e., uncertain, summary judgments. This weakness would be most pronounced in the residual-content evaluation, because that task involved aggregating the largest amount of content. Residual content was rated of uncertain validity in four of the five guidelines.

Aggregating large amounts of content is a weakness shared by all the topics we evaluated. However, it may not fully explain why our panelists rated so many of the physical modality topics of uncertain validity. The panelists reached similar conclusions for the two broad categories of treatment (lumbar spine and shoulder problems) and the one discrete diagnosis (carpal tunnel syndrome), which suggests that the ratings were uncertain for reasons other than aggregation.

Third, to our knowledge, no methods for evaluating clinical content have been validated to date. We borrowed from validated methods to the degree possible, but the main premise of our evaluation, using an expert panel to assess and compare multiple medical treatment guidelines, has not been described in the published literature.

Our findings, analysis, and input from stakeholders together inform our recommendations to the state, which are presented in Chapter Nine.

CHAPTER SEVEN

Stakeholder Issues and Concerns

Stakeholder Experiences with Interim Use of the ACOEM Guidelines

As discussed in Chapter Two, the California Labor Code requires an employer to pay for all medical care reasonably required to cure or relieve the effects of a worker's injury or illness. Recent legislation repealed a presumption of correctness accorded the treating physician that care is medically necessary; the new legislation established the ACOEM guidelines as presumptively correct regarding the extent and scope of medical treatment as of March 31, 2004, and until the AD issues a utilization schedule. The presumption affects the burden of proof and is rebuttable by "a preponderance of evidence establishing that a variance from the guidelines is reasonably required." For injuries not covered by the ACOEM guidelines, care is to be in accordance with "other evidence-based medical treatment guidelines recognized by the national medical community and that are scientifically based."

Implementation of the ACOEM guidelines as the presumptively correct standard to define reasonably required care is only one of a series of changes under way in the workers' compensation program. Another important change, effective January 1, 2005, gives employers the option of establishing a medical network of providers to care for injured workers for the entire duration of treatment. Treatment by medical network providers is to be in accordance with the ACOEM guidelines or the utilization schedule issued by the AD, as appropriate. In conjunction with another study task, examining the cost and quality issues affecting medical care provided to injured workers in California and the likely impact of the recent legislative changes, we conducted a series of interviews with stakeholders in the medical care provided injured workers. In this section, we discuss the findings from the interviews, which focused on stakeholder experiences during the early stages of implementation of the ACOEM guidelines. We believe that the themes emerging from these interviews inform policy and process issues that the AD may wish to consider in adopting a utilization schedule. Findings on other issues are presented in a separate report on the medical treatment study.

Methodology

Our interviewees included practicing physicians and practitioners in different special-ties that treat injured workers; applicants' attorneys and worker advocates; individu-als employed by payors to perform utilization review (UR) and claims administra-tion; government officials, including workers' compensation judges; and other persons generally knowledgeable about California workers' compensation issues. We used a semistructured interview technique to ask about the interviewees' perceptions of

- The strengths and weaknesses of the California workers' compensation program, with particular attention to cost-driver and quality issues.
- The likely impact of the recent legislative changes on incentives to deliver high-quality care in an efficient manner.
- Additional changes that should be made in the way care is delivered to injured workers in California.
- Particular aspects of the system that should be monitored closely.

To date, we have conducted 18 individual and group interviews, and we will continue to interview in connection with other study tasks. We started with a list of individuals and organizations that were recommended by either CHSWC or experts in occupational medicine as being knowledgeable stakeholders in California workers' compensation. We expanded the interviews to include others who expressed particu-lar interest in the medical treatment study and a desire to provide information on their particular experiences. Thus, the interviewees did not represent a random sam-ple of California stakeholders, but rather a spectrum of key informants with different perspectives and concerns. Not all of the interviews touched on implementation of the ACOEM guidelines. However, we found that most interviewees brought up these guidelines during the interview and that the medical network issues were of far less interest at the time, perhaps because the formal rulemaking process to implement the medical network provisions of SB 899 had not begun. The interviews were con-ducted from June to October 2004, so the findings reflect early experiences with the ACOEM guidelines, and some comments may become less relevant as workers, pro-viders, and payors alike gain familiarity with the guidelines and a history of Workers Compensation Appeal Board rulings is available to aid interpretation of how the guidelines should be applied. The interviews also took place before the AD issued regulations implementing the new statutory provisions affecting UR procedures; some issues that were raised in the interviews may be clarified when the regulations are issued.

Common Themes in the Interviews

The issues that were raised in the interviews can be categorized into two main groups:

- How the ACOEM guidelines are applied in UR to determine whether care is reasonably required.
- The UR process and procedures, including timeliness, reviewer credentials and training, and quality of explanations of denials.

While some themes expressed in the interviews are specific to the ACOEM guidelines, e.g., particular treatment areas that are not addressed, the responses raise generic issues that would be relevant if the AD were to adopt any of the guideline sets evaluated in this study.

How the ACOEM Guidelines Are Applied. There was general consensus that the use of evidence-based guidelines to define care reasonably required to cure or relieve an injured worker has the long-run potential to improve quality of care; however, the most common theme raised by the interviewees concerned the rigidity with which the guidelines are applied. Providers (including those selected by employers) and representatives for injured workers were consistently concerned that practice guidelines were being treated as "law," with no room for professional judgment in determining medically appropriate care based on particular patient needs. One interviewee noted that the medical-necessity definition had gone from "anything goes" to very stringent rules and that it will take a while to work out the right balance between applying those rules and allowing individual considerations. Another interviewee suggested that the guidelines should include space for clinical judgment, but it should be a narrow space.

Interviewees expressed concern that the burden of proof to rebut the ACOEM guidelines ("preponderance of evidence") is onerous, because evidence for frequency and duration is limited and many practice guidelines are consensus-based. Even when there is evidence to support a particular therapeutic approach, putting that evidence together is very time-consuming for a practicing physician, and while the care is reimbursable, the incremental effort of gathering evidence is not.

Stakeholders from the payor community were very supportive of having medical necessity defined by evidence-based guidelines, but the interviews revealed that in the absence of regulatory guidance, the stakeholders have taken different approaches in applying the guidelines. The ACOEM guidelines identify treatments that do not have evidence to support their use, and one payor is denying these treatments unless the physician provides documented evidence that the services are medically necessary. Another payor indicated that its UR physicians were reviewing these services and approving or denying them based on consultation with the primary physician.

Providers and payors alike noted that the ACOEM guidelines were developed as practice guidelines and that there is a need to translate them into UR criteria, including establishing the frequency and duration of care. Concern was also expressed that guidelines are directed to the primary-care physician caring for a worker at the acute stage of an injury, and they do not adequately address chronic conditions, particularly pain management. Other areas of particular concern that the interviewees highlighted were chiropractic services, physical and occupational medicine, acupuncture, devices, and new technologies. Several interviewees indicated that clarification is needed regarding when the guidelines apply and when they do not; in the view of these interviewees, even if the guidelines were not developed for chronic care, specific aspects of them are nevertheless applicable to the chronic stage of care. Payors in particular would like to see the guidelines expanded to cover all common conditions. In the interim, for conditions that are not addressed by the guidelines, payors appeared to have different interpretations of who should bear the burden of proof regarding whether a service is medically necessary, the treating physician or the payor.

UR Process and Procedures. Concerns were expressed that some payors are reviewing virtually all care and that because of the increased workload and the lack of familiarity with the guidelines, UR backlogs had developed that were creating delays in treatment and return to work. Payors had different interpretations regarding whether the law required that all care be reviewed for consistency with the ACOEM guidelines or whether discretionary review confined primarily to high-cost treatment and/or physicians with high utilization patterns was allowed.

According to providers, applicants' attorneys, and a workers' compensation appeals judge, the payors are taking a hard line, and as a result, almost every plan of treatment is contested. A common comment was that UR physicians are not willing to "step back" from the guidelines when the proposed care is medically necessary. Some interviewees noted that decisions to deny are not sufficiently explained, with the rationale often being "not supported by ACOEM," without further explanation or clear articulation of why the care is not reasonable. An applicant's attorney indicated that he was relying almost exclusively on the expedited hearing process to resolve medical treatment disputes.

Several interviewees questioned the qualifications and experience of the UR physicians and suggested that their credentials and credibility should be monitored. Concern was frequently expressed that the physicians making UR decisions were from out of state, had unknown credentials, and were not familiar with local medical practices. A common argument among non-primary-care physicians was that peer review should be required, i.e., UR physicians should be credentialed in the area they are reviewing. Particular concerns were expressed in this regard by orthopedic surgeons, chiropractors, therapists, and acupuncturists.

Concerns were also expressed that claims adjusters typically have no medical training, making review of cases for consistency with the ACOEM guidelines problematic and time-consuming, at least in the early stages of implementation. Claims adjusters have the authority to approve care consistent with the guidelines but can no longer modify the plan of treatment, as they could under the old rules, and must refer these cases to UR. An interviewee from the payor community suggested that in addition to increasing the backlog of cases handled by UR physicians, the policy has substantially increased the cost of performing UR and may lead to less UR in the future.

The UR provisions require a reply within five days for prospective review after all necessary information is received, and they allow no more than 14 days to respond. Payors noted that meeting these timelines during the ACOEM implementation phase has been a challenge but that review time has shortened as familiarity with the guidelines has increased. Implementing the ACOEM guidelines involved a "big learning curve" that required a major effort to train claims adjusters. Providers and applicants' attorneys consistently expressed concern with early decisions, using terms such as "inconsistent" and "capricious." Providers noted that it takes longer to get treatment decisions for workers' compensation claimants than for non-occupational health cases, with one interviewee noting that there should be a default policy if the decision is not timely; e.g., if the adjuster fails to respond within ten days, the treatment plan is deemed to be accepted.

Interviewees also cited a number of systemic problems. These include

- The challenges posed by the complexity of the different medical delivery models with different utilization and dispute-resolution processes, particularly after the medical networks become operational.
- The incentives and accountability for payors to make timely and appropriate decisions on medical treatment.
- The level of distrust and contention in the system.

Summary of Stakeholder Meeting on Guideline Implementation Issues

After the clinical evaluation of the five guideline sets was completed, we invited selected stakeholders to a meeting to share our findings to date and to obtain their input on implementation issues raised during the clinical evaluation and our ongoing stakeholder interviews. Most of the participants were representatives of stakeholder organizations that were suggested to us by CHSWC, some of whom had also been included in the interviews. Participants represented a variety of stakeholder perspectives: labor, applicants' attorneys, physicians and other practitioners, payors, and self-insured employers. The participants are listed in Appendix G. We deliberately kept the group small to facilitate a full and open exchange of viewpoints.

Participants were given in advance a set of discussion questions that we planned to use to focus the discussion on major implementation issues. The questions covered five issue areas:

1. Guideline set vs. a patchwork of guidelines
2. Topical gaps in the guidelines
3. Lack of relevant research
4. Exceptions to the guidelines
5. Updating and implementing revised guidelines

The discussion questions are reproduced in Appendix H. While all five areas were addressed at some point during the discussion, the participants spent most of the time on the issue of how the shortcomings in the ACOEM guidelines should be handled or, more specifically, how the AD could address the topical areas that need improvement. These included the areas that the clinical panel identified as being of uncertain validity (spinal fusion surgeries and the physical modalities), as well as other areas identified through the stakeholder interviews as being problematic because they were not addressed or were not addressed well (acupuncture, chronic care and pain management, devices, emerging technology, home health care, durable medical equipment, toxicology). At the end of the discussion period, each participant was asked to summarize what he or she considered the most important implementation issue.

The discussion revealed general agreement that the long-term goal should be to take the best guideline available for each topic area and patch them together into a single coherent set of guidelines, but there were differing viewpoints about the best mechanism for reaching that goal and the policies that should be adopted in the interim.

Payors tended to favor "staying the course" until a more valid and comprehensive guideline set could be developed. They noted that the ACOEM guidelines had just been implemented and that additional time is needed both to work out the ACOEM issues and to consider carefully the consistency and administrative issues that might arise with using multiple guidelines.

Other participants tended to favor adopting guidelines from different developers but suggested different interim strategies, ranging from using the AAOS guidelines for spinal surgery to adopting multiple guidelines as long as they meet some minimum criteria, such as listing in the National Guideline Clearinghouse or adoption by specialty societies. Longer-term strategies involved evaluating existing guidelines for other topical areas and working toward a comprehensive, consistent guideline set, using a multidisciplinary group of evaluators. These participants were concerned about the potential detrimental impact on workers of using guidelines of uncertain validity. Considerations that seemed to affect the viewpoints of these participants on the range of options for using multiple guidelines included whether a focus on the most common tests and therapies would be sufficient for specific industries, whether the state has the resources to develop and maintain quality guidelines, whether multiple guidelines are likely to raise serious conflicts and inconsistencies, the burden of proving that care that is not addressed by the guidelines is reasonably required, and the short statutory time frame allowed for the AD to consider the issues and adopt guidelines.

Other observations made by one or more participants included the following:

- The regulations implementing the new UR provisions might address some of the issues being experienced with the ACOEM guidelines, such as latitude for the UR physician to supplement ACOEM with other guidelines.
- The ACOEM guidelines were not written for UR, but were designed to guide physicians on treatment. One of the weaknesses of the guidelines is the absence of information on treatment modalities such as acupuncture. Another is a lack of specificity.
- More flexibility is needed in applying the guidelines in the UR process to allow for deviation based on professional judgment.

CHAPTER EIGHT

Application of the Guidelines to Determine Whether Care Is Reasonably Required

This chapter discusses some of the major issues concerning the way the utilization schedule adopted by the AD is applied during initial claims adjudication to determine whether care is reasonably required to cure or relieve the effects of a worker's injury or illness. We drew on the findings and clinical panel discussion from Chapter Six and the themes raised by stakeholders summarized in Chapter Seven to identify the issues and potential options. We supplement those findings with illustrative examples of how the issues have been addressed by other workers' compensation programs that might serve as a model for California. Our intent is to pose the questions, consider some of the possible options, discuss the advantages and disadvantages of those options, and, where possible, identify "best practices" that warrant further investigation. We do not attempt to provide answers to all of the questions. The issues are classified into two broad categories:

- How the utilization schedule is applied as the presumptively correct standard for care
- Processes and procedures used in UM

One of the most important questions motivating this study is whether the state should adopt as its utilization schedule a patchwork of guidelines from multiple developers or a guideline set from a single developer. We address this issue in the next chapter and present our conclusions and recommendations. The issues discussed below are relevant regardless of which option is selected.

How the Utilization Schedule Is Applied as the Presumptively Correct Standard

What Policies Should Apply to Topical Gaps?

The California Labor Code requires that the utilization schedule adopted by the AD "address, at a minimum, the frequency, duration, intensity, and appropriateness of all treatment procedures and modalities commonly performed in workers' compensation cases." As discussed in earlier chapters, all of the guideline sets that we evaluated have topical gaps for common workers' compensation conditions. Further, even if a patchwork of guidelines were used to cover additional common and costly conditions, the breadth of work-related injuries ensures that additional topical gaps will continue to exist. The California Labor Code provides some guidance for such situations:

> §4604.5. (g) For all injuries not covered by the American College of Occupational and Environmental Medicine Occupational Medicine Practice Guidelines or official utilization schedule after adoption pursuant to Section 5307.27, authorized treatment shall be in accordance with other evidence-based medical treatment guidelines generally recognized by the medical community.

Thus, the Labor Code contemplates the use of "other evidence-based medical treatment guidelines generally recognized by the medical community" if a condition or modality is not covered by the utilization schedule. The statutory language raises several potential issues that warrant consideration and clarification in the rulemaking process:

- What constitutes "evidence-based medical treatment guidelines generally recognized by the medical community"?
- What policies might be considered to reduce the likelihood of dueling guidelines for particular tests or therapies?
- What policies might be considered to address situations where there are no generally recognized evidence-based guidelines?
- Who has the burden of proof when the test or treatment is not covered by the utilization schedule?

Defining Evidence-Based Treatment Guidelines. Defining "evidence-based guidelines generally recognized by the medical community" as guidelines listed in the National Guideline Clearinghouse would ensure that the development methods for the guidelines have been externally reviewed and meet minimum standards. The National Guideline Clearinghouse standards are similar to but less detailed than those we used in our technical review (see Figure 8.1).

The advantage of defining evidence-based treatment guidelines as those guidelines listed in the National Guideline Clearinghouse is that the topical gaps would be filled, where applicable, with clinical guidelines meeting basic quality standards for development. Guidelines in the National Guideline Clearinghouse are also likely to have substantial credibility among clinicians. Because many of the National Guideline Clearinghouse guidelines are free, users would not be required to pay for multiple proprietary guidelines, and the basis for decisionmaking would be widely avail-

Figure 8.1
Criteria for National Guideline Clearinghouse Listing

For a clinical practice guideline to be considered for the National Guideline Clearinghouse, it must meet these criteria:

- The guideline must contain systematically developed recommendations, strategies, or other information to assist health care decisionmaking in specific clinical circumstances.
- The guideline must have been produced under the auspices of a relevant professional organization (e.g., medical specialty society, government agency, health care organization, or health plan).
- The guideline development process must have included a verifiable, systematic literature search and review of existing evidence published in peer-reviewed journals.
- The guideline must be current and the most recent version (i.e., developed, reviewed, or revised within the last 5 years).

SOURCE: National Guideline Clearinghouse, 2004.

able. Another advantage of using the National Guideline Clearinghouse listing is that the guideline developers have already done the literature review and have added expert opinion as necessary to address specific clinical questions.

There are some drawbacks, however, to using the National Guideline Clearinghouse to address topical gaps in the utilization schedule. The most important of these is that there is no guarantee that the highest-quality guideline would be selected. Not all evidence-based guidelines are listed in the National Guideline Clearinghouse—for example, of the five guideline sets we evaluated, only the AAOS, ODG, and Intracorp guidelines are listed. Moreover, no clinical evaluation of the guidelines is required before listing in the National Guideline Clearinghouse. Our findings from the current study suggest that both a technical evaluation and a clinical evaluation are needed to identify high-quality guidelines.

An alternative to using guidelines listed by the National Guideline Clearinghouse would be to establish a minimum standard for technical quality that a guideline would need to meet in order to be considered evidence-based. Both the National Guideline Clearinghouse standards and the AGREE instrument illustrate the type of criteria that could be used for this purpose. This alternative would create an administrative hurdle that developers would have to overcome before a guideline could be used to support treatment determinations. However, it might enable high-quality guidelines not listed by the National Guideline Clearinghouse to be used. As discussed below, the burden of making this assessment is more appropriately placed on the payor than on the provider caring for the injured worker.

Evaluating Dueling Guidelines. Issues in filling topical gaps arise when two or more evidence-based guidelines "generally recognized by the medical community" are in conflict. This is an important short-term issue that should become less important if the guidelines adopted by the AD become more comprehensive over time.

One approach would be to leave the resolution of such cases to the appeals process. However, this would be likely to result in administrative burdens and delays in medical treatment that might be avoided if regulatory guidance were provided.

Existing clinical guidelines provide useful information about evidence and opinions surrounding particular clinical decisions; however, the strength of evidence used to justify a guideline's recommendations should be considered in making decisions, not just whether or not the evidence was a guideline. Guidelines should be seen as a way of answering clinical questions and presenting evidence together with expert opinion; they should not be seen as evidence in and of themselves. A hierarchy of evidence, such as the AHCPR hierarchy (see Table 2.1), could be used to assess the relative strength of the evidence that supports dueling guidelines. Other systems for grading the strength of evidence, including checklist approaches, have been evaluated and might be candidates for adoption (West et al., 2002). As discussed below, the same hierarchy could be used in instances where there are no evidence-based guidelines to inform a treatment recommendation.

The disadvantage of using a hierarchy of evidence is that it assumes that all evidence was produced with the same rigorous attention to accepted methodological standards; this is not necessarily the case. For example, a systematic review or meta-analysis of randomized controlled trials, which is generally regarded as the highest level of evidence, may have biased reporting and constitute weaker evidence than a well-designed and reported randomized clinical trial. Further, a system for grading evidence cannot completely resolve the tradeoff between types of studies. One type, the randomized clinical trial, is best suited for examining the efficacy of a therapy under ideal circumstances, which means using carefully selected patients. Other types of studies, such as observational studies, are best for evaluating how well a therapy performs in the real world when provided to a large and diverse group of patients (West et al., 2002).

No Evidence-Based Medical Treatment Guidelines. The Labor Code does not explicitly address what will be assumed to be presumptively correct if there are no evidence-based medical treatment guidelines covering a topical gap. Consideration should be given to clarifying how medical-necessity determinations should be made when there are no relevant "evidence-based" guidelines but (1) there is other evidence addressing the test or therapy, or (2) there is no evidence-based literature addressing the topical area.

The Labor Code establishes the "preponderance of scientific medical evidence establishing a variance from the guidelines" as the burden of proof for rebutting the presumption (L.C. §4604.5) for the guidelines issued by the AD. It would be reasonable for other evidence to be considered when there are no relevant "evidence-based" guidelines to inform the treatment decision. However, we assume that where there are no guidelines, relevant evidence will be brought into discussion in a piecemeal fashion, and it is unlikely that a formal, exhaustive, systematic literature review will be performed for most UM decisions or in the dispute-resolution process. A hierarchy of evidence might be considered as a mechanism to provide some order to the determination process and to reduce disputes.

Unfortunately, there are many clinical circumstances for which evidence-based medicine cannot define *appropriate treatment*. Risks and potential benefits are often unclear because published evidence is equivocal, of poor quality, or entirely absent. Also, evidence that may appear incontrovertible to one party may lack credibility for another. Such situations are difficult to resolve and undoubtedly result in many disputes over the plan of treatment for an injured worker. Clarification of the standard to be used in these cases would be helpful in reducing disputes, particularly disputes over whether and under what circumstances expert opinion is to be considered as evidence. In the ACHCPR hierarchy of evidence, for example, opinions and clinical experience of respected authorities are recognized as the lowest level of evidence (AHCPR, 1999). Clarification regarding whether expert opinion constitutes evidence would be helpful even if a hierarchy of evidence were not adopted.

Burden of Proof. In our stakeholder interviews (see Chapter Seven), we heard several anecdotes in which payors had used topical gaps in the ACOEM guidelines to deny care that might otherwise have been considered appropriate and necessary. The underlying issue, which should be clarified in the implementing regulations, is whether the provider or the payor should have the burden of proof when a test or therapy is not addressed by the utilization schedule adopted by the AD. At a minimum, the implementing regulations should proscribe payors from denying care simply on the basis that the topic area is not included in the adopted guideline set.

There are several reasons why it would be appropriate to place the burden of proof on the payor rather than the provider in establishing that treatment not addressed by the adopted guidelines is "reasonably required." First, treating physicians will have examined and evaluated the injured worker and, provided the physicians have adequate expertise for the clinical situation, should be in the best position to make clinical decisions on behalf of the worker. In this regard, we note that with the establishment of medical networks, employers will have greater control over physician choice, and there should be fewer questions about whether the treating physician is providing inappropriate care; such circumstances may promote underuse of necessary care rather than overuse of inappropriate services.

Second, while an overall objective should be to increase the practice of evidence-based medicine, it is not reasonable to expect a practicing provider to survey and evaluate the medical literature supporting a treatment plan for a particular patient. A theme raised in the stakeholder interviews and meeting was that it is quite burdensome for a provider to document on a case-by-case basis whether a test or therapy is supported by evidence. Placing the burden of proof on the provider might make it more difficult for patients to access practitioners who furnish well-established therapies not addressed by the adopted guidelines.

Third, as discussed in greater detail later in this chapter, UM will reduce costs in the California workers' compensation system only if it is a cost-effective activity itself. The return on investment from UR is much lower for inexpensive or rare clinical situations than it is for costly and common ones. The cost of reviewing the cases can, in some circumstances, exceed the financial savings realized from denying inappropriate care. If the burden of proof rests with the provider, the payor bears little cost in challenging the appropriateness of care and has an incentive to review virtually all care. This passes some of the cost of UM on to the provider and may make providers reluctant to assume the burden of proof. Unless the provider is willing to challenge denials of care and assume the burden of proof, patients may be denied appropriate care.

If the burden of proof were on the payor, UR would be limited to the official utilization schedule and any topical gaps the payor determines would be cost-effective to address. Payors could use existing evidence-based guidelines, develop their own treatment policies or guidelines based on evidence, review care falling into topical gaps on a case-by-case basis, or employ other UM strategies. If denial decisions were based on high-quality evidence, payors might find treating clinicians more willing to accept the denials and should find themselves on relatively solid ground if the denials are appealed. Placing the burden of proof on the payor has the potential to increase the practice of evidence-based medicine while reducing administrative burden and the amount of contention in the system.

Topical gaps that have not been addressed by published clinical research pose a particular problem in establishing burden of proof. Clarification of whether and under what circumstances expert opinion should be considered evidence would establish more-consistent policies for handling these topic areas.

Some well-established therapies lack a supporting body of evidence-based studies; for these therapies, additional policies might be needed to implement UR procedures. For example, the guidelines for acupuncture to treat low back pain adopted by Colorado's Division of Workers' Compensation place the burden of proof on the provider to show functional improvement within a limited total number of treatments (see Figure 8.2). The guidelines use a comparable approach with respect to active and passive physical/occupational therapy and spinal manipulation (State of Colorado, 2001).

Topical gaps also include new and emerging technologies, which may not have been addressed in the medical literature. This is a somewhat different issue than that of well-established therapies, because the question of whether the test or treatment is cause the question of whether the test or treatment is safe and effective is uninformed by either evidence or experience. Additional guidance may be needed regarding whether these services should be considered "reasonably required" as a general policy.

Figure 8.2
Excerpt from the Colorado Medical Treatment Guideline for Acupuncture

Acupuncture is the insertion and removal of filiform needles to stimulate acupoints (acupuncture points). Needles may be inserted, manipulated and retained for a period of time. Acupuncture can be used to reduce pain, reduce inflammation, increase blood flow, increase range of motion, decrease the side effect of medication-induced nausea, promote relaxation in an anxious patient, and reduce muscle spasm.

Indications include joint pain, joint stiffness, soft tissue pain and inflammation, paresthesia, post-surgical pain relief, muscle spasm, and scar tissue pain.

(1) Time to produce effect: 3 to 6 treatments
(2) Frequency: 1 to 3 times per week
(3) Optimum duration: 1 to 2 months
(4) Maximum duration: 14 treatments

SOURCE: State of Colorado, 2001.

During RAND's 20-year history of examining the appropriateness of a variety of therapies, RAND researchers have considered overuse synonymous with providing inappropriate care—that is, care for which the risks to the patient exceed the potential benefits, irrespective of costs. The RAND researchers do not consider it overuse when care of uncertain benefit is provided, because such a large proportion of medical care falls into this category—as much as 32 percent of care for common, well-studied therapies is of uncertain benefit (Naylor, 1995; Park et al., 1989). The percentage is likely to be much higher for uncommon, emerging, or complementary/alternative therapies. Applying RAND's historical interpretations to the California workers' compensation system, we believe the goal of using evidence-based medicine to define *reasonably required care* is to limit the provision of clearly inappropriate care, i.e., care for which the risks to the patient exceed the potential benefits.

Risks could exceed potential benefits for two reasons: (1) the risks of the care are substantial and the potential benefits modest, or (2) there are no potential benefits (all tests and therapies have some risks, however small). If either of these is true, care is inappropriate and should not be provided. The state might want to clarify that for care not addressed by the adopted utilization schedule, judgments of risks and potential benefits can be based on published evidence, ranked according to quality, or, in the absence of such evidence, expert opinion. In most instances, the burden should be on the payor to demonstrate that care is inappropriate. Special policies may be warranted for tests or therapies for which there is no evidence in the medical literature.

What Policies Should Apply to Unusual Cases?

The most common theme raised during our stakeholder interviews was that the ACOEM guidelines were developed as guidelines but were being implemented as stringent rules without consideration of a particular patient's unique circumstances. At the stakeholder meeting, some participants voiced the need for recognition that some care might fall outside the utilization schedule because of unusual patient needs; however, there were no specific suggestions regarding the policy or mechanism that could be used to accomplish this.

Labor Code §4604.5(a) states that the presumption that the utilization schedule adopted by the AD is presumptively correct "is rebuttable and may be controverted by a preponderance of the evidence establishing that a variance from the guidelines is reasonably required to cure and relieve the employee from the effects of his or her injury." This section is problematic because exceptions to medical guidelines are generally needed in unusual clinical circumstances that may not be addressed by the literature. The burden of proof may not be surmountable in most cases where a variance is appropriate, unless further guidance is provided in the implementing regulations. Because the guidelines are presumptively correct throughout the appeals process, consideration should be given to embedding an exceptions policy into the guidelines or the regulations. The key policy questions are

- What is the appropriate balance between applying the guidelines and recognizing exceptions?
- How might this policy be incorporated into the guidelines?

The content and validity of the adopted guidelines, and the degree to which they differentiate between different strata of patients and particular therapies, will affect how often exceptions might be judged appropriate. In the final analysis, payors should base decisions on medical judgments about a particular patient's needs rather than on whether the adopted guideline specifies the particular medical circumstances warranting an exception. Thus, the AD should consider specifically authorizing payors to use medical judgment in deciding whether care at variance with the adopted guidelines should be allowed. We found that there was confusion among our stakeholder interviewees regarding whether payors had latitude to approve care outside the ACOEM guidelines.

L.C. §4604.5(b), which allows an employer to authorize in writing additional visits beyond the 24-visit limitation for chiropractic, physical therapy, and occupational therapy services, might serve as a model in this regard. The language and process that other workers' compensation programs use to allow deviation from their treatment guidelines warrant further consideration as well. For example, Colorado's treatment guidelines explicitly recognize that from 3 to 10 percent of injured workers will not recover within the specified timelines and specify that additional treatment will require "clear documentation by the authorized treating practitioner focusing on objective functional gains afforded by additional treatment and impact upon prognosis." (State of Colorado, 2001).

How Should the Guidelines Be Updated?

The state needs to have a process for updating the guidelines and keeping them current with advances in evidence-based medicine. An important policy issue is how much oversight the state should exercise over the updating process. If the updated guideline is to be "presumptively correct" under the law, the state has a duty to ensure that the modifications are appropriate and acceptable for injured workers in California. Otherwise, the guideline developers will wield an inappropriate amount of decisionmaking authority in the California workers' compensation system.

In addition, the updating issue is complicated by potentially different updating cycles:

- All five of the guideline sets we evaluated are updated at least every three years. It is possible that with either a comprehensive guideline set or a patchwork of guidelines, individual guidelines for particular topic areas might be updated on different timetables. It will be challenging for the state to establish an appropriate balance between using the most current guideline available for a topic and assuring consistency in the guidelines across topics.
- A three-year updating cycle is more relaxed than the annual evaluation required for UR criteria (L.C. §4610). To avoid misunderstandings and inconsistencies, the UR regulations should set out what is expected in the annual updates as well as any periodic revisions needed to conform to revisions in the guidelines adopted by the AD.

One option would be to update the California workers' compensation guidelines independent of the actual updating cycle used by the guideline developers. The guidelines adopted by the AD would thus remain "frozen" until revised by the AD. This would allow the state to provide maximum oversight over the guidelines, but it has the disadvantage of delaying implementation of more-current evidence-based guidelines.

A second option would be to require that the guidelines be automatically updated on a rolling basis when released by the developer (e.g., 60 days after release of the updated guideline to allow payors time to implement the change) unless the AD took action to delay implementation. This would preserve the state's oversight obligations and would allow consideration of the internal consistency of guidelines, without slowing the implementation of appropriate updates. There are tradeoffs in the administrative burdens associated with this approach. Payors would face the burden of revising their utilization criteria on an ongoing basis, but the piecemeal changes might pose fewer training and implementation challenges than absorbing a number of changes simultaneously would. A variant of this option would be to provide for automatic updates on a regular basis (e.g., any revised guidelines that have been issued before November 1 of a given year would be effective January 1 of the next year unless the AD took action to delay the effective date).

Another option would be to allow for automatic "rolling updates" but to require a comprehensive periodic review (e.g., every three years) of the guidelines for internal consistency, validity, and comprehensiveness,. A multidisciplinary panel of expert clinicians could oversee this process, and using a nationally representative panel would help ensure that the guidelines are judged according to a national standard of care, as required by the Labor Code. This option has the advantage of providing for both timely updates and state oversight. It also explicitly incorporates a process for determining whether guidelines from other developers should be considered for adoption by the California program. And it provides a mechanism for addressing situations where guideline developers neglect to maintain the currency and appropriateness of their guidelines.

Regardless of the mechanism that is used to update the guidelines, clarification will be needed regarding whether a revised guideline applies to care provided to an injured worker whose claim predates the issuance of the revised guideline. Although the policy could require that injured workers remain subject to the guideline that was in effect when they filed their initial claim, this would basically ensure that workers with long-term, complex health conditions will eventually receive out-of-date care. It may be preferable to require providers to use the most up-to-date guideline available at the time new or modified treatment plans are being formulated.

What Is the Relationship Between Guidelines and Utilization Review Criteria?

Labor Code §5307.27 requires that the AD adopt a utilization schedule that addresses "at a minimum, the frequency, duration, intensity, and appropriateness of all treatment procedures and modalities commonly performed in workers' compensation cases. " As indicated earlier in this report, the term *utilization schedule* does not have a commonly accepted definition, and it is not clear whether the law intends that nationally recognized evidence-based standards of care be issued as a utilization schedule in a one-step process or a two-step process. Given the ambiguity in the language, we surveyed both practice guidelines and guidelines developed to assist payor decisions. As discussed in Chapter Five, our technical review of the guidelines included an assessment of applicability, i.e., whether the guideline developers discuss the potential organizational barriers and cost implications of applying the recommendations and whether the guideline includes criteria for monitoring and review. Three of the five guideline sets that we evaluated, including ACOEM, received low applicability scores, meaning that they did not address implementation issues very well.

The low applicability ratings are also consistent with a theme raised in both our stakeholder interviews and the stakeholder meeting, namely, that the ACOEM guidelines were developed as practice guidelines and should be translated for UR purposes. Interviewees questioned whether payors have the latitude to do this themselves, i.e., regulatory guidance is needed clarifying whether the language in L.C. §4610 requiring that the utilization-criteria review "be consistent" with the utilization schedule means that the criteria must be identical to the utilization schedule or that it can be developed from the utilization schedule by providing more explicit review criteria for identifying inappropriate care.

Users may find it difficult to use clinical guidelines for UR, because those guidelines generally are written not with the intent of eliminating inappropriate care but with the intent of recommending appropriate care. In short, clinical guidelines may not address utilization questions adequately. Researchers have found it possible to translate clinical guidelines for the purpose of measuring underuse, but they report that the process was difficult and time-consuming. We did not identify a method for translating clinical guidelines into utilization (i.e., overuse) criteria, but we suspect that this may be difficult to do. Further, the translation process itself creates the opportunity for variable interpretations and increases the likelihood of disputes.

To assure greater consistency across payors and to reduce the overall administrative burden, the state may wish to consider as a long-term strategy supporting the development and maintenance of UR criteria focusing on the most important cost drivers for medical care furnished to injured workers. In addition to ensuring consistency, this approach would place any resultant guidelines in the public domain, where they would be readily available for multiple purposes. However, it places a considerably higher ongoing administrative burden on the state than does the current approach, i.e., relying on existing guidelines developed by others. Rather than covering all aspects of care for a clinical problem, as guidelines do, the utilization criteria should be targeted to clinical circumstances relevant to determining the appropriateness of specific tests and therapies and should focus on common injuries that frequently lead to costly and inappropriate services. The utilization criteria should be usable for either prospective or retrospective assessments of appropriateness, because UM in the California system involves both types of activities. The criteria should use precise language so that they will be interpreted consistently.

Consideration of Nonclinical Factors in Providing Care

The state may want to consider clarifying whether payors can take nonclinical considerations into account in determining whether a particular therapy is "reasonably required." These could include, for example, whether the care is furnished in the least costly setting, e.g., inpatient vs. outpatient, and whether there are less costly but equally effective therapies that should be tried first.

Processes and Procedures Used in Utilization Management

Medical treatment guidelines provide the foundation for the delivery of evidence-based medical care to injured workers in California. As outlined in SB 228, these treatment guidelines are to serve as the basis for establishing a utilization schedule, which, in turn, will guide the development of review criteria to be used for UM. Translating the clinical information and evidence incorporated in a utilization schedule into an operational system that can manage medical care delivered to injured workers will present significant challenges.

A central feature of the implementation process will be the development of effective UM processes that provide the mechanism for determining whether medical care for a given patient is appropriate and consistent with treatment guidelines. Although widely used by health care payors and health plans, UM has come under criticism from the provider community because it increases providers' administrative burden and decreases their autonomy. Nonetheless, it continues to be used and, in fact, is becoming more widespread (Mays, Claxton, and White, 2004).

Critical to the success of any UM system will be provider training, finding ways to increase provider acceptance of the system, and the easing of administrative burden. This section discusses important implementation issues regarding UM and its use within the context of the California workers' compensation system. Because of the many unknowns regarding the design and implementation of a UM system and the very early development stage of implementing the SB 228 provisions, we refrain from making explicit recommendations. Rather, we highlight key issues related to implementation that will need to be addressed at a later stage.

Disseminating Guidelines to Providers

One of the early implementation tasks will be to disseminate the treatment guidelines to providers who deliver care through the California workers' compensation system. As discussed in a recent review article, "Dissemination is the active process of making information available to the target audience. It is the process by which knowledge is made accessible or available to a specific audience" (Bauchner and Simpson, 1998). Dissemination of treatment guidelines remains a challenge, particularly if the guidelines are proprietary and have copyright protections. No single strategy has yet been identified that offers clear benefits over other strategies. Common methods of disseminating treatment guidelines include direct mailing to providers, publication in newsletters or journals, electronic dissemination, educational or continuing-medical-education (CME) activities, and providing information about guidelines to patients and consumers (Graham et al., 2003). Several of these methods may be proscribed if the AD adopts a utilization schedule based on proprietary guidelines. Studies suggest that direct mailing alone has significant shortcomings and is not effective in promoting guideline adoption (Grol and Grimshaw, 1999).

Because most physicians treat relatively few injured workers, they may be less motivated to comply with the treatment guidelines. Making the guidelines readily available is therefore especially important. Posting the treatment guidelines on the Internet, as is done in the state of Washington, would be one useful mode of dissemination, but it may be precluded by copyright protections. Even when guideline dissemination is followed by multifaceted interventions, improvements in care processes have been found to be modest (Davis and Taylor-Vaisey, 1997).

The regulatory circumstances under which the treatment guidelines and the utilization schedule will be implemented for the California workers' compensation system are very different from the prevailing conditions described in the literature. Because compliance with the utilization schedule will be directly linked to payment, providers should be strongly motivated to conform to the guidelines. Effective dissemination will nevertheless be important for promoting acceptance of the guidelines and enhancing their usefulness.

In sum, developing an effective strategy for disseminating the treatment guidelines will require attention and planning. Assuming that providers will obtain the guidelines on their own initiative is unlikely to advance the goal of improving quality by encouraging the provision of evidence-based medical care. Active local implementation involving training and provider education may be needed.

Training and Educating Providers to Improve Compliance with Treatment Guidelines

Despite the multitude of treatment guidelines developed over the past two decades, there is limited evidence of successful implementation leading to changes in routine medical practice. What the literature clearly indicates is that passive dissemination does not facilitate adoption and use of treatment guidelines (Smith, 2000; Davis et al., 1995; Matowe et al., 2002). More-active implementation strategies are needed. But such strategies can involve considerable expense, raising the question of the relative costs and benefits of different strategies.

The literature on clinical guidelines is voluminous, indicating the emphasis placed on this important aspect of medical care. Indeed, during the past 15 years, more than 4,000 articles have been published and indexed in MEDLINE. We confine ourselves to noting several useful published overviews of research pertaining to implementing treatment guidelines and to highlighting several relevant points concerning approaches to implementation. Published reviews of studies concerning interventions designed to change physician behavior are described in a special issue of *Medical Care* published in August 2001. The issue also includes findings. Other overviews of published articles on translating guidelines into practice and the efficacy of educational interventions to change providers' practice behaviors include Graham et al., 2003; Davis and Taylor-Vaisey, 1997; Smith, 2000; Sohn, Ismail, and Tellez, 2004; Davis, 1998; and Grimshaw et al., 2004.

Studies of treatment-guideline dissemination processes have reported mixed findings. In their review of 59 studies, Grimshaw and Russell note that 55 studies reported statistically significant improvements in care processes (Grimshaw and Russell, 1993). However, the effect was highly variable. In general, limited dissemination approaches—in particular, direct mailings or traditional CME—appear to have little effect on the likelihood of guideline adoption (Davis and Taylor-Vaisey, 1997). The main advantage of these approaches is resource savings. Stronger interventions, such as reminder systems, academic detailing, and multiple interventions, produce better results but usually cost more (Davis et al., 1995; Wensing, van der Weijden, and Grol, 1998). Reminder systems may be worth special consideration in light of the fact that, as noted earlier, most physicians treat relatively few workers' compensation patients. In the state of Washington, the substantial majority of physicians who participate in the workers' compensation system treat fewer than 20 workers' compensation patients per year. One would expect a similar situation in California. Under these conditions, reminders may be particularly effective for reinforcing the use of guidelines.

Under the California workers' compensation reform, employers will be able to direct injured workers to physician networks. The establishment of these networks may facilitate the dissemination of the treatment guidelines. For example, academic detailing, or making outreach visits to physicians' offices, has been shown to be effective, especially if it involves opinion leaders—educationally influential and respected clinicians (Davis and Taylor-Vaisey, 1997; Lomas et al., 1989). While it would be too costly to perform academic detailing on an individual-physician basis, it may be affordable at a network level.

Another factor shown to influence guideline implementation is the complexity of the guideline itself. Guidelines that are relatively uncomplicated appear to have a better chance of being adopted by providers (Rogers, 1995; Grilli and Lomas, 1994).

The specific form of provider training and education most appropriate for implementing the treatment guidelines within California's workers' compensation system will have to be determined on the basis of a careful assessment of the practitioner community and other relevant factors. In regard to this assessment, we make two points, based upon our review of the literature. First, many factors affect the implementation of treatment guidelines. Conducting a pilot test as part of the assessment process prior to full-scale implementation of any new guidelines may be very useful. This would allow different implementation approaches to be evaluated and would improve understanding of key factors that may be critical to success. Second, as noted earlier, the costs and benefits of different implementation approaches will vary significantly. As with many things in life, "cheaper is not always better." Stronger implementation approaches will cost more but are likely to yield better results.

Utilization Management Processes

As discussed earlier, using UM to review and authorize medical care for designated conditions and procedures will require the development of review criteria, based on the utilization schedule to be established. At this early juncture, there are many unknowns and questions regarding how this complex task will proceed. Here, we highlight a few of the important issues related to UM.

As noted in an earlier IOM report (Gray and Field, 1989), UM programs and procedures vary greatly. One of the distinguishing features of workers' compensation is its focus on disability prevention and management. By law, injured workers are eligible to receive compensation for lost wages due to work-related injuries. Disability (wage replacement) payments in California constitute about 50 percent of total workers' compensation expenditures. Effective UM requires more than the application of review criteria to authorize medical care. Case management, disease management, and related activities should be performed to limit disability and improve the workers' chances of returning to meaningful employment. In workers' compensation, a small group (<10 percent) of claimants account for the great majority of costs. Typically, these injured workers have not suffered severe injuries but, rather, have received medical care that has been poorly managed (Wickizer et al., 2001). Such care often leads to costly and prolonged disability.

Performing UM activities requires, at a minimum, competent, well-trained staff and integrated data systems. Unfortunately, organizations performing UM for workers' compensation too often have neither (Gray and Field, 1989). Much of the resistance to UM within the provider community has resulted from inefficiency and long delays in obtaining approval for requested medical care. Many of these problems can be directly linked to the lack of adequately trained staff or to outdated information systems. Additional problems arise when appeal procedures for denied care are not well defined and when appeals are not acted upon promptly and fairly.

It will be important for organizations conducting UM to adhere to standards regarding structures and performance processes. URAC (also known as the American Accreditation HealthCare Commission), a national accrediting organization established in 1990, provides accreditation for UM organizations.

Recently, URAC developed accreditation standards for workers' compensation UM. These standards are comprehensive and attempt to ensure that organizations performing UM have the necessary structures and processes to promote high-quality care and preserve patient rights. Currently, URAC is finalizing updated standards (version 3.0) for workers' compensation UM. Six workers' compensation programs recognize some form of URAC accreditation in their UM standards. In the District of Columbia, quality oversight for care management is provided by requiring that workers' compensation system UM organizations be accredited by URAC and adhere to URAC standards (URAC, 2000).

Promoting provider acceptance of UM will also be important. One reason for resentment and criticism of UM by physicians is the perception that the decisions made to authorize care are arbitrary and place cost considerations above quality-of-care considerations. The underlying problem is often a lack of understanding regarding the review criteria used to authorize medical care and the perception that the review criteria have, at best, limited clinical validity (Wickizer and Lessler, 2002). While it may not be possible to completely overcome provider resistance to having medical care subject to review and authorization, making the review criteria transparent will certainly help. Presumably, the review criteria developed to authorize care will be directly linked to the treatment guidelines via the utilization schedule. This should significantly enhance the credibility of the review criteria and thereby promote provider acceptance. The systematic, detailed process used to evaluate the suitability of the guidelines for the California workers' compensation system may pay important dividends in terms of demonstrating the state's commitment to establishing an evidence-based UM system.

Easing Provider Administrative Burden

Arguably, the single most frustrating aspect of UM for providers is the increase in paperwork and administrative burden (Wickizer and Lessler, 2002). Gaining acceptance by the provider community will require reducing the administrative burden associated with UM as much as possible. There are several ways this could be accomplished. First, as noted above, it is important that UM organizations have competent, well-trained staff, efficient appeals processes, updated integrated information systems, and appropriate quality management. Policies that encourage organizations that review medical care for workers' compensation to obtain URAC accreditation will help to ensure that UM procedures are performed efficiently and effectively.

Second, it may be possible to use a targeting approach to perform UM instead of requiring all providers to obtain prospective authorization for medical treatments. Ongoing analyses of the workers' compensation utilization management system in the state of Washington indicate that a sizable proportion of physicians in any given year have no requests for medical care denied (Wickizer et al., 2004). This suggests that it may be feasible to use a targeted approach to UM. Physicians whose denial rates fall below some defined threshold for designated procedures could be exempted from prospective review or could be reviewed on a more limited basis. Other physicians would be subject to normal prospective review. This approach would have the benefit of reducing provider administrative burden and system administrative costs while giving providers a strong incentive to comply with the treatment guidelines. Preliminary analysis from Washington indicates that such an approach might reduce the proportion of physicians subject to continual prospective review by as much as 40 to 50 percent, reducing the number of reviews performed by as much as 60 percent.

Use of a targeted approach to UM requires an ability to "profile" providers with regard to denial rates. Because many providers treat few workers' compensation patients, and there are multiple payors, it may be difficult to use a targeting approach that depends upon reliable assessment of denial rates at the individual-provider level. However, this could be accomplished at the network level, since many more patients would be treated within any given network. Using such an approach may have the added benefit of motivating providers active in workers' compensation health care delivery to join networks. As more medical care is delivered through these networks, it should be possible to improve clinical management and thereby achieve improved outcomes.

Toward a Best-Practice System

The California workers' compensation system has the opportunity to establish an innovative system that supports the delivery of evidence-based medical care. An important part of this system will be the performance of UM. Ensuring that UM responds to the needs of stakeholders, including patients, providers, and employers, will be critical to the success of the workers' compensation reform effort. This means developing a UM system that is efficient and transparent in its authorization process and that, to the extent possible, eases providers' administrative burden. The goal of this system should be not to deny care, but to support the delivery and management of appropriate evidence-based medical treatment aimed at restoring the injured worker to full function and returning him or her to back to work in a timely manner.

CHAPTER NINE

Conclusion

The California legislature recently passed a series of initiatives aimed at reducing costs and inappropriate medical care utilization in the workers' compensation system (AB 749 [Calderon], 2002; SB 228 [Alarcón], 2003; SB 899 [Poochigan], 2004). The initiatives centered on the use of medical treatment guidelines, i.e., systematically developed statements that assist in making decisions about appropriate health care for specific clinical circumstances (discussed in Chapter Two). SB 228, passed in 2003, adopted a temporary set of guidelines for treatment of injured workers; SB 899 further defined the guidelines. The temporary guidelines—developed by the American College of Occupational and Environmental Medicine (ACOEM) (ACOEM, 2003)—remain presumptively correct unless and until the Administrative Director (AD) of the Division of Workers' Compensation (DWC) chooses to replace or modify them.

According to the legislated plan, after suitable study and evaluation, either the ACOEM guidelines or a better alternative will be adopted. The AD of DWC was required to adopt a utilization schedule based on these guidelines by December 1, 2004. The specific language of the revised Labor Code mandates the use of evidence-based standards:

> §77.5(a): [The Commission on Health and Safety and Workers' Compensation (CHSWC)] shall conduct a survey and evaluation of evidence-based, peer-reviewed, nationally recognized standards of care.

> §5307.27: [The Administrative Director of the Division of Workers' Compensation (DWC), in consultation with CHSWC, will adopt after public hearings] a medical treatment utilization schedule, that shall incorporate the evidence-based, peer-reviewed, nationally recognized standards of care recommended by the Commission . . . and that shall address, at a minimum, the frequency, duration, intensity, and appropriateness of all treatment procedures and modalities commonly performed in workers' compensation cases.

Overview of Methods and Findings

This legislation guided our study. Our approach was to identify guidelines addressing work-related injuries, screen those guidelines using multiple criteria, and evaluate the guidelines that met our criteria. It is important to note that we accomplished these objectives in a very limited time frame and within a limited scope; because of these constraints, we were not able to conduct an independent review of the clinical literature or develop new guidelines.

Using multiple complementary search strategies, we identified 72 guidelines that address work-related injuries (the full list of these guidelines is given in Appendix A). From these, we selected a subset for further evaluation on the basis of quality (the guidelines had to be evidence-based, peer-reviewed, nationally recognized, developed with a multidisciplinary process, and reviewed at least every three years) and cost (less than $500 per individual user). In hopes of identifying a single set of guidelines that could address the most common and costly tests and therapies in a rigorous, evidence-based fashion, we focused on evaluating guideline sets, rather than evaluating multiple separate guidelines. Resource limitations precluded us from pursuing both approaches simultaneously. Five sets of guidelines met the selection criteria:

1. AAOS—Clinical Guidelines by the American Academy of Orthopedic Surgeons
2. ACOEM—American College of Occupational and Environmental Medicine Occupational Medicine Practice Guidelines
3. Intracorp—Optimal Treatment Guidelines, part of Intracorp Clinical Guidelines Tool®
4. McKesson—McKesson/InterQual Care Management Criteria and Clinical Evidence Summaries
5. ODG—Official Disability Guidelines: Treatment in Workers Comp, by Work-Loss Data Institute

We compared these guidelines in terms of technical quality and clinical content. All five guidelines performed reasonably well on technical quality, although AAOS, ACOEM, and Intracorp addressed implementation issues poorly.

We convened a multidisciplinary panel of expert clinicians to evaluate the comprehensiveness and validity of guideline content addressing utilization decisions—specifically, appropriateness and quantity of care. The panelists found that, with some exceptions, the five selected guideline sets address the appropriateness of surgical therapies well, but they were frequently uncertain about whether the guidelines address the appropriateness of physical modalities in a comprehensive and valid manner. The panelists came to similar conclusions regarding the quantity of care for physical modalities. The remaining content within each guideline set was rated either not comprehensive (AAOS) or of uncertain validity (the rest). The panelists preferred the ACOEM guideline set and judged its entire content to be valid, although they were uncertain about whether it was evidence-based or comprehensive. The results of the clinical evaluation are summarized in Table 9.1.

Comments during the meeting revealed that most panelists believed the five guideline sets "barely meet standards," they preferred specialty society guidelines over those marketed for utilization management (UM) purposes because the latter seem too "proscriptive," and some panelists knew little of the published literature addressing the physical modalities.

The clinical evaluations were limited by the fact that we aggregated substantial amounts of clinical material and asked panelists to make summary judgments, which may have increased the likelihood of uncertain or intermediate ratings. Also, our lack of a literature review may have had a similar effect on ratings, particularly in areas with which panelists were relatively unfamiliar.

Despite our methodological limitations, the clinical content evaluation leads us to the following conclusions:

- All five guideline sets appear far less than ideal; in the words of the panelists, they barely meet standards.
- The clinical panel preferred the ACOEM guidelines to the alternatives and considered them valid but of uncertain comprehensiveness in the entire-content rating.

Table 9.1
Clinical Evaluation Summary: Panelists' Assessment of Comprehensiveness and Validity

	AAOS	ACOEM	Intracorp	McKesson	ODG
Appropriateness					
Surgery	2 of 4 topics	3 of 4 topics	1 of 4 topics	3 of 4 topics	2 of 4 topics
Physical therapy and chiropractic	0 of 6 topics	1 of 6 topics	0 of 6 topics	2 of 6 topics	2 of 6 topics
Residual Content					
	Not comprehensive	Validity uncertain	Validity uncertain	Validity uncertain	Validity uncertain
Entire Content					
Rating	**Valid**, comprehensiveness uncertain	**Valid**, comprehensiveness uncertain	Not valid	Validity uncertain	Validity uncertain
Median rank	4	**1**	3	2	2

- The ACOEM guideline set addresses cost-driver surgical topics well for three of the four therapies the panel rated.
- The ACOEM guideline set does not address lumbar spinal fusion well, but the AAOS guideline set does.
- The ACOEM guidelines do not appear to address physical modalities very well, but the other four guidelines do little better.
- Panelists were uncertain whether the residual content within the ACOEM guideline set is valid, but the other four sets do little better.

Analysis and Recommendations

Guideline Evaluation

This study was commissioned to inform a policy decision as to which, if any, of the five guideline sets is of high enough quality to serve as a basis for a "presumptively correct" utilization schedule under the law in the California. The clinical panelists' conclusion in this regard was that all five guideline sets were far from ideal and that substantial improvement would be desirable. Panelists found the McKesson and ODG guideline sets, both marketed for UM purposes, to be of uncertain validity overall, and they commented that these guidelines were overly proscriptive, meaning that they limited clinical options to a degree that made the panelists uncomfortable. The ACOEM and AAOS guideline sets were judged valid in the overall evaluation, and the ACOEM was seen as preferable to the currently available alternatives. Thus, the results of the clinical content evaluation indicate that there is no reason for the state to choose another guideline set to replace the ACOEM at this time.

However, we found the ACOEM guidelines to be of uneven quality. While surgical topics were relatively well addressed, panelists were uncertain whether content was valid for physical modalities or other common and costly therapies. This suggests that CHSWC and the AD of DWC should carefully consider which guidelines should be presumptively correct under the law for the short, intermediate, and longer term.

For the short term, it is important to consider which topics are most important for the utilization schedule to address and whether the ACOEM does so in a valid and comprehensive fashion. Priority topic areas include the following tests and therapies that are common and costly in the California workers' compensation system: MRI of the spine, spinal injections, spinal surgeries, physical therapy, chiropractic manipulation, surgery for carpal tunnel syndrome and related conditions, shoulder surgery, and knee surgery. Of these, surgical procedures are generally the most costly per service and should therefore take precedence in the selection of a guideline. Inappropriate surgical procedures can also involve substantial risks for patients, much greater risks than those posed by the other priority therapies. We believe, for these reasons, that the utilization schedule should adequately address the appropriateness of surgical procedures, particularly lumbar spinal decompression procedures, lumbar spinal fusion procedures, carpal tunnel surgery, shoulder surgery, and knee surgery. Spinal fusion surgery is especially controversial and risky, and its use is rapidly increasing in the United States (Deyo, Nachemson, and Mirza, 2004; Lipson, 2004); therefore, it warrants additional emphasis.

The ACOEM guideline set appears valid and comprehensive in defining appropriateness for three of the four procedures our panel considered in detail: lumbar spinal decompression surgery, carpal tunnel surgery, and shoulder surgery. Although we did not ask the panelists to address knee surgery in detail, our internal clinical team found that the five guideline sets make relatively similar recommendations regarding this therapy. Thus, the ACOEM guideline set addresses all five of the most important surgical topics and appears to do so well for three of the four we studied. It would be reasonable to generalize our findings and surmise that the ACOEM addresses most surgical topics well.

Only the AAOS guideline appears valid and comprehensive in addressing the fourth procedure we studied, lumbar spinal fusion surgery. The AAOS guideline was also valid and comprehensive for lumbar spinal decompression surgery. Because the failure to address lumbar spinal fusion surgery well is an important weakness in the ACOEM guidelines, the AAOS guideline could supplement or replace it for that topic or for spinal surgery in general. An occupational medicine physician on our team reviewed the ACOEM and AAOS guidelines for contradictory recommendations regarding lumbar spinal fusion surgery and found several differences. He noted that the AAOS guideline seems to find fusion surgery appropriate for a wider range of clinical circumstances than the ACOEM guideline does. Although further examination of the issue is warranted, it appears reasonable to replace the ACOEM content with the AAOS content for at least lumbar spinal fusion surgery.

Physical modalities are less costly per service and less risky than surgical procedures, but it is important that a utilization schedule cover them because high utilization rates for these services contribute substantially to medical care costs in the California workers' compensation system. A few experts have told us that some employees do not return to work while they are receiving ongoing physical modalities; if this is true, these modalities may also indirectly increase work-related disability payments. Physical therapy and chiropractic manipulation are currently provided for a wide variety of injuries, including those of the spine, wrist, knee, hip, and shoulder. A utilization schedule that defines both appropriateness and quantity of care for the physical modalities addressing these body regions would therefore be helpful.

Determining the appropriateness of manipulation also has important implications for the role of California chiropractors in workers' compensation cases, because chiropractors are supposed to provide physical therapy modalities only "in the course of chiropractic manipulations and/or adjustments" (California Laws and Regulations Relating to the Practice of Chiropractic).

Although it is clearly important to define appropriateness for physical modalities, this was found to be a consistent area of weakness across all of the guidelines. The ACOEM guideline could be strengthened somewhat by adding complementary sections from the ODG guideline—specifically, those for carpal tunnel syndrome—but physical modalities would still remain an area of weakness.

Defining quantity of care for physical modalities was another consistent area of weakness found across the five guideline sets; however, this may not be a critical problem. The recent legislation defines quantity of care for physical therapy and chiropractic manipulation: patients can have up to 24 visits per injury. Whether this cap is high, low, or adequate may be subject to debate, but it does provide the state with some means of controlling the frequency and duration of use of these services.

Stakeholder Experiences and Opinions

Through interviews with stakeholders, we learned about difficulties that have arisen during the interim period in which the ACOEM guidelines have been presumptively correct under California law. Payors appear to be interpreting and applying the guidelines inconsistently. Moreover, payors appear uncertain about which topics the ACOEM set covers in enough detail to determine appropriateness of care. Finally, the guidelines have sometimes been applied to topics they address minimally or not at all.

After concluding our evaluation of the five guidelines, we presented our findings to a group of California stakeholders. Most of them appeared to agree that none of the five comprehensive guideline sets is going to be adequate for the California workers' compensation system and that, ultimately, the state may need to either develop a set of guidelines from scratch or patch together existing guidelines into a coherent and consistent set. The stakeholders suggested a range of interim strategies that should be considered until a more valid and comprehensive guideline set can be developed. Payor and employer representatives tended to favor "staying the course"; others representing providers and injured workers suggested that the interim strategy should be either to fill in the most critical gaps with selected guidelines or to adopt multiple and potentially overlapping guidelines that meet minimum criteria.

The Labor Code provides that evidence-based guidelines will be used to make medical-necessity determinations for topical areas not covered by the utilization schedule adopted by the AD. As a result, little would be gained by an "across-the-board" adoption of multiple guidelines that meet minimum screening criteria as an interim strategy. Indeed, adopting multiple guidelines without evaluating the quality of those guidelines and eliminating inconsistencies in overlapping content area could create more issues than it resolves. At the same time, there is a pressing need to address some areas that are not addressed well in the comprehensive guideline sets (e.g., the physical modalities) and those that are addressed minimally or not at all (e.g., acupuncture).

Recommendations

Based on our study findings and stakeholder considerations, we make the following recommendations to the state.

Short Term (After December 1, 2004)

1. The panelists preferred the ACOEM guideline set to the alternatives, and it is already in use in the California workers' compensation system; therefore, there is **no reason to switch to a different comprehensive guideline set at this time.**

2. ACOEM content was rated comprehensive and valid for three of the four surgical topics considered, and our evaluation methods appeared successful for these topics; therefore, **the state can confidently implement the ACOEM guideline for carpal tunnel surgery, shoulder surgery, and lumbar spinal decompression surgery.**

3. Because spinal fusion surgery is especially controversial and risky, and its use is rapidly increasing in the United States (Deyo, Nachemson, and Mirza, 2004; Lipson, 2004), it warrants additional emphasis. The AAOS content was rated comprehensive and valid for this procedure as well as for lumbar spinal decompression surgery; therefore, **the state can confidently implement the AAOS guideline for lumbar spinal fusion surgeries and, if convenient, for lumbar spinal decompression surgery.**

4. The ACOEM guideline set performed well for three of the four categories of surgery we evaluated. Generalizing these findings to other surgical topics would be reasonable; therefore, **the state could implement the ACOEM guideline for other surgical topics.**

5. Our findings question the validity of the ACOEM guidelines for the physical modalities and the residual content, but our evaluation methods appeared to have important limitations for these areas; therefore, **we are not confident that the ACOEM guideline is valid for nonsurgical topics.** Deciding whether or not to continue using ACOEM for nonsurgical topics as an interim strategy remains a policy matter.

    a. We recommend that to identify high-quality guidelines for the nonsurgical topics, the state proceed with the intermediate-term solutions described below as quickly as possible.

6. **We suggest implementing regulations to clarify the following issues:**

    a. Stakeholder interviews suggest that payors in the California workers' compensation system are applying the ACOEM guidelines inconsistently and sometimes for topics the guidelines do not address or address only minimally;

therefore, **we recommend that the state issue regulations clarifying the topics for which the adopted guidelines should apply,** e.g., acupuncture, chronic conditions, and other topics that may not be covered well by the ACOEM guidelines.

    b. **For topics to which the adopted guideline does not apply, the state should clarify who bears the burden of proof for establishing appropriateness of care.**

    c. **For topics not covered by the adopted guideline and throughout the claims adjudication process, the state should consider testing the use of a defined hierarchy to weigh relative strengths of evidence.**

    d. Because the medical literature addressing appropriateness and quantity of care may be very limited for some physical modalities and other tests and therapies, some guideline content will include a component of expert opinion; therefore, **the state should clarify whether expert opinion constitutes an acceptable form of evidence** within "evidence-based, peer-reviewed, nationally recognized standards of care."

    e. Our stakeholder interviews suggest that payors are uncertain whether they have the authority to approve exceptions to the guidelines for patients with unusual medical needs. Therefore, **the state should consider specifically authorizing payors to use medical judgment in deciding whether care at variance with the adopted guidelines should be allowed.**

Intermediate Term

1. If the state wishes to develop a patchwork of existing guidelines addressing work-related injuries, our research suggests the following priority topic areas: **physical therapy of the spine and extremities, chiropractic manipulation of the spine and extremities, spinal and paraspinal injection procedures, magnetic resonance imaging (MRI) of the spine, chronic pain, occupational therapy, devices and new technologies, and acupuncture.**

    a. When guidelines within a patchwork have overlapping content, the state may want to identify and resolve conflicting recommendations.

2. Because high scores in the technical evaluation were not associated with high evaluations by expert clinicians, **we recommend that future evaluations of existing medical treatment guidelines include a clinical evaluation component.** Specifically, we recommend against adopting guidelines solely on the basis of acceptance by the National Guideline Clearinghouse or a similar standard, because this criterion ensures only the technical quality of listed guidelines.

3. If the state wishes to employ the clinical evaluation method we developed for multiple future analyses, **we suggest that at least one analysis should involve an attempt to confirm the validity of the clinical evaluation method,** including determining the effect of a literature review on panel findings.

4. Lack of a comprehensive literature review appeared to be a major limitation in our evaluation of content addressing the physical modalities; therefore, **future evaluations addressing the physical modalities should include a comprehensive literature review.**

Longer Term

1. Our technical evaluation revealed that ACOEM and AAOS developers did a poor job of considering implementation issues, and our stakeholder interviews indicated that payors are applying the ACOEM guidelines in an inconsistent fashion. Therefore, **we recommend that the state develop a consistent set of utilization criteria (i.e., overuse criteria) to be used by all payors.**
    a. Rather than covering all aspects of care for a clinical problem, as guidelines do, these utilization criteria should be targeted to clinical circumstances relevant to determining the appropriateness of specific tests and therapies.
    b. Rather than defining appropriateness for all tests and therapies provided to injured workers, the criteria should focus on common injuries that frequently lead to costly and inappropriate services.
    c. The utilization criteria should be usable for either prospective or retrospective assessments of appropriateness, because utilization management in the California workers' compensation system involves both types of activities.
    d. The criteria should use precise language so that they will be interpreted consistently.

2. Another task within this project addresses development of a quality-monitoring system for California workers' compensation. Underuse of medical care is one important component of quality; therefore, the state may need to develop criteria for measuring it. **Developing the overuse and underuse criteria at the same time would be resource-efficient.**

3. There are two basic ways the state could develop overuse and underuse criteria:
    a. **The criteria could be developed from existing guidelines,** such as the ACOEM, AAOS, or any other guidelines judged valid in future studies. However,
        i. We are unaware of a reliable, validated method for developing overuse criteria from existing medical treatment guidelines. We suspect that it may be difficult to develop overuse criteria from guidelines written for clinicians, e.g., the ACOEM and AAOS guidelines. Development of overuse criteria would probably require input from the original developers or a comprehensive literature review or both.
        ii. Researchers have developed a reliable, validated method for developing underuse criteria from existing medical treatment guidelines.
    a. **The criteria could be developed from the literature and expert opinion,** without the intermediate step of developing or selecting guidelines.

i. The RAND/UCLA Appropriateness Method (RAM) was specifically designed to develop overuse and underuse criteria based on the literature and expert opinion. Although future researchers could select a different method for developing the criteria, RAM has been validated and used extensively. RAND has put this method into the public domain by publishing a detailed manual (Fitch et al., 2001).

APPENDIX A
Identified Guidelines That Address Work-Related Injuries

Source	Guideline Title	Date[a]
AHCPR	Acute Pain Management	1992
AHCPR	Lower Back Problems in Adults	1994
AHCPR	Management of Cancer Pain	1994
ALA-California /California Thoracic Society	ATS Guidelines for the Evaluation of Impairment/ Disability in Patients with Asthma	1993
ALA-California/California Thoracic Society	ATS Standards for the Diagnosis and Care of Patients with Chronic Obstructive Pulmonary Disease	1995
American Academy of Neurology, American Academy of Physical Medicine and Rehabilitation, American Association of Electrodiagnostic Medicine	Practice Parameter: Electrodiagnostic Studies in Carpal Tunnel Syndrome	2002
American Academy of Orthopaedic Surgeons	Guidelines and Support Documents for Hip Pain, Knee Injury, Knee Osteoarthritis, Low Back Pain/Sciatica, Shoulder Pain and Wrist Pain	2001–2003
American College of Occupational and Environmental Medicine	Occupational Medicine Practice Guidelines, Second Edition	2004
American College of Radiology	ACR Appropriateness Criteria™ for Acute Hand and Wrist Trauma	2001
American College of Radiology	ACR Appropriateness Criteria™ for Chronic Elbow Pain	2001
American College of Radiology	ACR Appropriateness Criteria™ for Acute Trauma to the Knee	2001
American College of Radiology	ACR Appropriateness Criteria™ for Suspected Cervical Spine Trauma	2002

Source	Guideline Title	Date[a]
American College of Radiology	ACR Appropriateness Criteria™ for Acute Hand and Wrist Trauma	2001
American Geriatric Society	The Management of Persistent Pain in Older Persons	2002
American Medical Directors Association	Pain Management in the Long-Term Care Setting	2003
American Orthopaedic Foot and Ankle Society (AOFAS)	The AOFAS Workers Compensation Manual	2003
American Pain Society	Pain in Osteoarthritis, Rheumatoid Arthritis, and Juvenile Chronic Arthritis	2002
American Physical Therapy Association, Philadelphia Panel	Philadelphia Panel Evidence-Based Clinical Practice Guidelines on Selected Rehabilitation Interventions for Knee Pain	2001
American Physical Therapy Association, Philadelphia Panel	Philadelphia Panel Evidence-Based Clinical Practice Guidelines on Selected Rehabilitation Interventions for Shoulder Pain	2001
American Physical Therapy Association, Philadelphia Panel	Philadelphia Panel Evidence-Based Clinical Practice Guidelines on Selected Rehabilitation Interventions for Low Back Pain	2001
American Physical Therapy Association, Philadelphia Panel	Philadelphia Panel Evidence-Based Clinical Practice Guidelines on Selected Rehabilitation Interventions for Neck Pain	2001
American Psychiatric Association	Practice Guidelines for the Treatment of Psychiatric Disorders	2004
American Society of Anesthesiologists	Practice Guidelines for Chronic Pain Management	1997
American Society of Interventional Pain Physicians (ASIPP)	ASIPP Evidence-Based Practice Guidelines for Interventional Techniques in the Management of Chronic Spinal Pain	2003

Source	Guideline Title	Date[a]
American Society of Interventional Pain Physicians (ASIPP)	Interventional Techniques in the Management of Chronic Pain, Part 2.0	2001
Association of Pain Management Anesthesiologists	Interventional Techniques in the Management of Chronic Pain, Part 1.0	2000
Brigham and Women's Hospital	Upper Extremity Musculoskeletal Disorders	2003
California Podiatric Medical Association	Clinical Practice Guidelines for the Diagnosis & Treatment of Heel Pain, Diabetic Foot Disorders, Diagnosis & Treatment of First Metatarsophalangeal Joint Disorders, Hammertoe Syndrome, RSD/Complex Regional Pain Syndrome, Treatment of Pressure Ulcers	1994–2003
California State Compensation Insurance Fund	Catastrophic Injury Treatment Guidelines & Protocols	1995–2001
Canadian Chiropractic Association	Clinical Guidelines for Chiropractic Practice in Canada (Glenerin Guidelines)	1993
Commonwealth of Massachusetts Department of Industrial Accidents	Massachusetts Treatment Guidelines	1993-2004
Council on Chiropractic Practice	Vertebral Subluxation in Chiropractic Practice	2003
Dutch Institute for Health Care Improvement	Guideline for the Diagnosis and Treatment of Specific Acute and Chronic Low Back Complaints	2004
Dutch National Institute of Allied Health Professions	Clinical Practice Guideline for the Physiotherapy of Patients with Whiplash-Associated Disorders	2001
EBI	Treatment Guidelines for Osteogenic Stimulators – Spinal and Nonspinal Applications	ND
Industrial Medical Council	Chiropractic Industrial Medical Council Guidelines (Neck, Low Back)	1997

Source	Guideline Title	Date[a]
Institute for Clinical Systems Improvement (ICSI)	Adult Low Back Pain	2003
Institute for Clinical Systems Improvement (ICSI)	Diagnosis and Treatment of Adult Degenerative Joint Disease (DJD) of the Knee	2003
Institute for Clinical Systems Improvement (ICSI)	Assessment and Management of Acute Pain	2004
International Chiropractic Association (ICA)	Recommended Protocols and Guidelines for the Practice of Chiropractic	1993
International Spinal Injection Society	Practice Guidelines for Spinal Diagnostic and Treatment Procedures	2003
International Spinal Injection Society	Practice Guidelines for Spinal Diagnostic and Treatment Procedures	2003
InterQual, McKesson	McKesson's QualityFirst® Workers' Compensation/ Disability Guidelines	2003
Intracorp	Optimal Treatment Guideline	2003
London, Royal College of General Practitioners	Clinical Guidelines for the Management of Acute Low Back Pain	2001
Medtronic Neurological	Neurostimulation	ND
Medtronic Neurological	Intrathecal Drug Delivery	ND
National Osteoporosis Foundation	Health Professional's Guide to Rehabilitation of the Patient with Osteoporosis	2003
North American Spine Society	Phase III Clinical Guidelines for Multidisciplinary Spine Care Specialists: Spinal Stenosis, Version 1.0.	2002
North American Spine Society	Phase III Clinical Guidelines for Multidisciplinary Spine Care Specialists: Unremitting Low Back Pain	2000

Source	Guideline Title	Date[a]
North American Spine Society	Phase III Clinical Guidelines for Multidisciplinary Spine Care Specialists: Spondylolysis, Lytic Spondylolisthesis and Degenerative Spondylolisthesis (SLD)	2000
Proceedings of the Mercy Center Consensus Conference, Gaithersburg MD	Guidelines for Chiropractic Quality Assurance and Practice Parameters	1993
Reflex Sympathetic Dystrophy Syndrome Association	Clinical Practice Guideline for the Diagnosis, Treatment, and Management of Reflex Sympathetic Dystrophy/ Complex Regional Pain Syndrome (RSD/CRPS) (second edition)	2002
State of Colorado	Colorado Workers' Compensation Rules of Procedure, Rule XVII: Medical Treatment Guidelines	1998–2003
State of Oklahoma	Oklahoma Treatment Guidelines	1997–2003
State of Oregon	Oregon Diagnosis and Treatment Guideline for Carpal Tunnel Syndrome	1997
State of Rhode Island	Rhode Island Administrative Filing of the Medical Treatment Protocols of the Medical Advisory Board of the Rhode Island Workers Compensation Court	1992–2004
State of West Virginia	West Virginia Workers' Compensation Treatment Guidelines	1995–2000
State of Wyoming	Wyoming Physical Therapy Utilization Guidelines for the Care and Treatment of Injured Workers	2002
The Council of Acupuncture and Oriental Medicine Associations, and Foundation for Acupuncture Research	Acupuncture and Electroacupuncture: Evidence-Based Treatment Guidelines 2004	2004
Unclear	Manipulation Under Anesthesia	ND
University of Iowa Gerontological Nursing Interventions Research Center	Acute Pain Management	1999

Source	Guideline Title	Date[a]
University of Michigan Health System	Knee Pain or Swelling: Acute or Chronic	2002
University of Michigan Health System	Acute Low Back Pain	2003
Veterans Health Administration	Clinical Practice Guidelines for the Management of Low Back Pain or Sciatica in the Primary Care Setting	1999
Veterans Health Administration and Department of Defense	Clinical Practice Guidelines for the Management of Postoperative Pain	2002
Veterans Health Administration and Department of Defense	Low Back Pain in the Primary Care Setting	1999
Washington State	Washington State Medical Treatment Guidelines	1988–1994
Wisconsin Medical Society	Wisconsin Guidelines for the Assessment and Management of Chronic Pain	2004
Work Loss Data Institute	ODG Treatment in Workers' Comp 2004	2003
WSIB (Workplace Safety & Insurance Board) of Ontario, Canada	Ontario Program of Care for Acute Low Back Injuries	2002
Wyoming Division of Workers' Safety and Compensation	Wyoming Chiropractic Utilization Guidelines for the Care and Treatment of Injured Workers	2002

ND = No date provided.

Publicly Posted Screening Criteria[1]

1. **Nationally recognized.** Any of the following:
   - Accepted by the National Guidelines Clearinghouse.
   - Published in a peer-reviewed U.S. medical journal.
   - Developed, endorsed, or disseminated by an organization based in two or more U.S. states.
   - Currently used by one or more U.S. state governments.
   - In wide use in two or more U.S. states.

2. **Current.** Developed, updated, or reviewed during the past three years.
   - When portions of a guideline are considered current, but other portions are not, only the portions considered current will be evaluated further.

3. **Comprehensive guideline sets are preferred.** Guideline sets that address two or more procedures and modalities performed for musculoskeletal injuries of the spine, the upper extremities, *and* the lower extremities.
   - Individual guidelines addressing one type of commonly performed procedure or modality will be included only if a minority of the comprehensive guideline sets meeting the screening criteria address that procedure or modality.

4. **Evidence-based, peer-reviewed.** Based, at a minimum, on a systematic review of literature published in medical journals included in the National Library of Medicine's MEDLINE.
   - Convincing evidence of a systematic review of the literature includes lists of search terms, inclusion and exclusion criteria, the number of articles identified by the search and the number meeting the inclusion criteria, a bibliography of literature
     selected for inclusion, and criteria for appraising the literature selected.

5. **Developed by a multidisciplinary clinical team.** Developed or reviewed by a multidisciplinary team including at least three major types of providers that care for injured workers:

---

[1] Posted on the California Department of Industrial Relations website.

- Family medicine physicians
- Internal medicine physicians
- General practitioners
- Occupational health specialists
- Orthopedic surgeons
- Neurosurgeons
- Physical medicine specialists
- Physical therapists
- Chiropractors
- Radiologists
- Neurologists
- Acupuncturists
- Others

Convincing evidence of a multidisciplinary clinical team includes the names and specialties of clinical-guideline developers and the dates on which guideline development meetings were held.

6. **Kept up to date.** Developers plan to update or review the guidelines at least every three years.
   - Convincing evidence includes a written attestation of this plan provided to RAND by August 9, 2004.

7. **Potentially open source.** Developers are considering making the guidelines available to the public at a cost of less than about $500 per individual user.
   - Convincing evidence includes a written attestation of this plan provided to RAND by August 9, 2004.

Selecting Clinical Panelists

Methods

Our objective was to convene a national panel of experts in musculoskeletal injuries, specifically, clinicians who were actively practicing at least 20 percent of the time and who had some experience treating injured workers. We sought the following types of practitioners: primary care physicians, occupational medicine specialists, physical medicine and rehabilitation specialists, radiologists, neurologists, orthopedic surgeons, neurosurgeons, physical therapists, and doctors of chiropractic.

To identify such individuals, we contacted relevant national specialty societies listed on the website of the American Medical Association: American Academy of Neurology, American Academy of Orthopaedic Surgeons, American Academy of Physical Medicine and Rehabilitation, American Association of Neurological Surgeons, American College of Occupational and Environmental Medicine, American College of Physicians/American Society for Internal Medicine, American Academy of Family Physicians, American College of Radiology, American Medical Association, Society for General Internal Medicine, American Orthopaedic Association, and Radiological Society of North America. To identify physical therapists, we contacted the American Physical Therapy Association. To identify chiropractors, we contacted the American Chiropractic Association, Council on Chiropractic Practice, and International Chiropractors Association. Eight societies representing a broad spectrum of providers caring for injured workers provided nominations. The only desired specialty that was not represented among our nominees was radiology.

After receiving the nominations, we contacted each nominee to determine his or her interest and potential availability for our panel date. We then requested curriculum vitae. We selected panelists on the basis of the following attributes: national balance (we wanted no more than about 20 percent of the panelists to be from California), diversity of practice setting (academic vs. nonacademic), evidence of leadership in their specialty, diversity of experience treating injured workers (from modest to substantial experience), and lack of direct involvement with any of the guidelines under review. We sought to have two panelists experienced in treatments not commonly ordered or provided by other panel members, in order to increase the discussion related to those topics. We wanted to have at least one person on the panel with experience in the methods of guideline development and at least one with extensive experience with the literature addressing musculoskeletal injuries. Experience with expert panels was a plus.

The most promising candidates were interviewed by telephone to determine relevant experience, attitude toward the use of evidence-based medicine for utilization management (UM) purposes, potential conflicts of interest, and self-described ability to function within a team. Because this last attribute is so central to the success of expert panels, we also contacted references before offering the nominees positions on the panel.

The final 11-member clinician panel comprised one general internal medicine physician, two occupational medicine physicians, one physical medicine and rehabilitation physician, one physical therapist, one neurologist also board-certified in pain management, two doctors of chiropractic medicine, two orthopedic surgeons, and one neurosurgeon. The panelists are listed in Table C.1.

Table C.1
Clinical Panelists

Name	Primary Specialty	Secondary Specialty	State	Practice Type
Bartleson, J. D.	Neurology	Pain management	Minnesota	Large group practice
Bernacki, Edward	Occupational medicine	Preventive medicine	Maryland	Academic, research and clinical
Blackett, Benjamin	Neurosurgery	Attorney at Law	Washington	Private practice, consulting
Brown, Sam	Physical therapy		Kentucky	Private practice
Christensen, Kim	Chiropractic		Washington	Academic, clinical
Hessl, Stephen	Occupational medicine	Internal medicine	Colorado	Private practice, previously academic, clinical, and administration
Leiner, John	Internal medicine		Virginia	Academic, clinical
Mandell, Peter	Orthopedics		California	Solo private practice
McClelland, George	Chiropractic	Acupuncture	Virginia	Private practice
Sandin, Karl	Physical medicine and rehabilitation		California	Private practice
Strain, Rick	Orthopedics		Florida	Private practice

Sample Rating Forms, Round One

This appendix presents samples of the forms that panelists used to rate the selected guideline sets in round one of the rating process.

Guideline Rating Form for Selected Topic

Rate all items. 1 = Lowest possible, 9 = Highest possible.

Comprehensive means addresses **appropriateness of physical therapy for lumbar spine** for most patients who might be considered candidates.

Valid means recommendations addressing **appropriateness of physical therapy for lumbar spine** are evidence-based or consistent with expert opinion.

	Comprehensive	Valid
ACOEM		
Ratings	1 2 3 4 5 6 7 8 9	1 2 3 4 5 6 7 8 9
Comments (optional)		
Intracorp		
Ratings	1 2 3 4 5 6 7 8 9	1 2 3 4 5 6 7 8 9
Comments (optional)		
McKesson		
Ratings	1 2 3 4 5 6 7 8 9	1 2 3 4 5 6 7 8 9
Comments (optional)		
ODG		
Ratings	1 2 3 4 5 6 7 8 9	1 2 3 4 5 6 7 8 9
Comments (optional)		
AAOS		
Ratings	1 2 3 4 5 6 7 8 9	1 2 3 4 5 6 7 8 9
Comments (optional)		

Topic: <u>Physical therapy for lumbar spine</u>   Round: <u>one</u>

Dimension: <u>Appropriateness</u>   Rater: <u>[rater]</u>

Guideline Rating Form for Selected Topic

Rate all items. 1 = Lowest possible, 9 = Highest possible.

Comprehensive means addresses **frequency, intensity, and duration of physical therapy for lumbar spine** for most patients who might be considered candidates.

Valid means recommendations addressing **frequency, intensity, and duration of physical therapy for lumbar spine** are evidence-based or consistent with expert opinion.

	Comprehensive	Valid
ACOEM		
Ratings	1 2 3 4 5 6 7 8 9	1 2 3 4 5 6 7 8 9
Comments (optional)		
Intracorp		
Ratings	1 2 3 4 5 6 7 8 9	1 2 3 4 5 6 7 8 9
Comments (optional)		
McKesson		
Ratings	1 2 3 4 5 6 7 8 9	1 2 3 4 5 6 7 8 9
Comments (optional)		
ODG		
Ratings	1 2 3 4 5 6 7 8 9	1 2 3 4 5 6 7 8 9
Comments (optional)		
AAOS		
Ratings	1 2 3 4 5 6 7 8 9	1 2 3 4 5 6 7 8 9
Comments (optional)		

Topic: <u>Physical therapy for lumbar spine</u>   Round: <u>one</u>
Dimension: <u>Frequency, intensity, and duration</u>   Rater: <u>[rater]</u>

Guideline Rating Form for Residual Content

Rate all items. Consider all content **excluding the selected topics above**.

Comprehensive means the residual content addresses **appropriateness, frequency, intensity, and duration for procedures and modalities that tend to be common and costly in workers' compensation systems.**

Valid means recommendations addressing **appropriateness, frequency, intensity, and duration for these procedures and modalities** are evidence-based or consistent with expert opinion.

	Comprehensive	Valid
ACOEM		
Ratings	1 2 3 4 5 6 7 8 9	1 2 3 4 5 6 7 8 9
Comments (optional)		
Intracorp		
Ratings	1 2 3 4 5 6 7 8 9	1 2 3 4 5 6 7 8 9
Comments (optional)		
McKesson		
Ratings	1 2 3 4 5 6 7 8 9	1 2 3 4 5 6 7 8 9
Comments (optional)		
ODG		
Ratings	1 2 3 4 5 6 7 8 9	1 2 3 4 5 6 7 8 9
Comments (optional)		
AAOS		
Ratings	1 2 3 4 5 6 7 8 9	1 2 3 4 5 6 7 8 9
Comments (optional)		

Topic: <u>Residual content</u>   Round: <u>one</u>
Dimension: <u>All</u>   Rater: <u>[rater]</u>

Summary Rating Form for Entire Guidelines

Rate all items. Consider all content **including the selected topics above**.

Comprehensive means the content addresses **appropriateness, frequency, intensity, and duration for procedures and modalities that tend to be common and costly in workers' compensation systems.**

Evidence-based means recommendations addressing **appropriateness, frequency, intensity, and duration for these procedures and modalities** are consistent with published, peer-reviewed medical literature ranked according to quality of evidence. Valid means evidence-based or consistent with expert opinion.

	Comprehensive	Valid
ACOEM		
Ratings	1 2 3 4 5 6 7 8 9	1 2 3 4 5 6 7 8 9
Comments (optional)		
Intracorp		
Ratings	1 2 3 4 5 6 7 8 9	1 2 3 4 5 6 7 8 9
Comments (optional)		
McKesson		
Ratings	1 2 3 4 5 6 7 8 9	1 2 3 4 5 6 7 8 9
Comments (optional)		
ODG		
Ratings	1 2 3 4 5 6 7 8 9	1 2 3 4 5 6 7 8 9
Comments (optional)		
AAOS		
Ratings	1 2 3 4 5 6 7 8 9	1 2 3 4 5 6 7 8 9
Comments (optional)		

Topic: _Entire content_   Round: _one_

Dimension: _All_   Rater: _[rater]_

Ranking Form for Entire Guidelines

Place a number next to each guideline indicating your ranking, based on your opinion of its relative comprehensiveness and validity. For example, circle 1 for your first choice, 2 for your second choice, etc.

ACOEM					
Ranking	1	2	3	4	5
Comments (optional)					

Intracorp					
Ranking	1	2	3	4	5
Comments (optional)					

McKesson					
Ranking	1	2	3	4	5
Comments (optional)					

ODG					
Ranking	1	2	3	4	5
Comments (optional)					

AAOS					
Ranking	1	2	3	4	5
Comments (optional)					

Topic: Entire content   Round: one
Dimension: All   Rater: [rater]

Clinical Panel Ratings, Round Two

How to read the tables in this appendix: The first row of numbers within each category (e.g., appropriateness) indicates how many panelists chose each possible response on the 1–9 scale shown below it. The second row of numbers represents the 1–9 scale. The third row shows the median response for the group, followed by mean absolute deviation and, for cases in which the median falls within either the 1–3 or 7–9 range, whether or not there was agreement within the group (ND = no disagreement).

COMPREHENSIVENESS	AAOS	ACOEM	Intracorp	McKesson	ODG
Lumbar Spine					
Physical Therapy					
Appropriateness	6.0 (1.5)	6.0 (0.7)	5.0 (1.7)	6.0 (1.1)	6.0 (1.4)
Quantity	3.0 (2.1)ND	4.0 (1.3)	7.0 (1.1)ND	6.0 (1.2)	6.0 (1.5)
Chiropractic					
Appropriateness	2.0 (1.2)ND	4.0 (1.3)	6.0 (1.1)	6.0 (1.5)	7.0 (1.3)ND
Quantity	1.0 (1.3)ND	3.0 (1.5)ND	7.0 (1.6)ND	6.0 (1.5)	6.0 (1.3)
Surgery-Decompression					
Appropriateness	7.0 (0.6)ND	7.0 (0.6)ND	7.0 (1.1)ND	7.0 (0.7)ND	6.0 (1.5)
Surgery-Fusion					
Appropriateness	7.0 (1.4)ND	7.0 (0.5)ND	4.0 (1.3)	7.0 (0.6)ND	7.0 (1.5)ND

Note: Each cell reports the distribution of ratings across the 1–9 scale together with the median and (interquartile range).

COMPREHENSIVENESS	AAOS	ACOEM	Intracorp	McKesson	ODG
Carpal Tunnel					
Physical Therapy					
Appropriateness	2 4 1 2 1 1 **1** 2 3 4 5 6 7 8 **9** 3.0 (1.6)ND	2 4 3 2 **1** 2 3 4 5 6 7 **89** 6.0 (0.8)	3 1 2 3 2 **1** 2 3 4 5 6 7 **89** 5.0 (1.3)	1 6 3 **1** 2 3 4 5 6 7 **89** 6.0 (0.8)	1 3 3 2 1 **1** 2 3 4 5 6 7 **89** 7.0 (1.3)ND
Quantity	2 6 1 1 **1** 2 3 4 5 6 7 8 **9** 2.0 (0.9)ND	4 5 2 **1** 2 3 4 5 6 7 8 **9** 3.0 (0.7)ND	2 1 1 5 2 **1** 2 3 4 5 6 7 **89** 7.0 (1.2)ND	1 1 2 3 3 **1** 2 3 4 5 6 7 **89** 6.0 (1.5)	1 1 2 4 3 **1** 2 3 4 5 6 7 **89** 5.0 (1.1)
Chiropractic					
Appropriateness	10 **1** 2 3 4 5 6 7 8 **9** 1.0 (0.5)ND	2 2 2 3 2 **1** 2 3 4 5 6 7 8 **9** 6.0 (2.0)	1 1 2 3 3 **1** 2 3 4 5 6 7 **89** 7.0 (2.0)ND	1 1 2 4 3 **1** 2 3 4 5 6 7 **89** 8.0 (1.6)ND	1 3 1 3 2 **1** 2 3 4 5 6 7 **89** 7.0 (1.8)ND
Quantity	10 **1** 2 3 4 5 6 7 8 **9** 1.0 (0.5)ND	1 1 1 2 5 **1** 2 3 4 5 6 7 8 **9** 8.0 (2.1)ND	1 1 2 4 1 2 **1** 2 3 4 5 6 7 **89** 7.0 (1.5)ND	1 1 5 2 1 **1** 2 3 4 5 6 7 **89** 8.0 (1.7)ND	4 1 1 3 1 1 **1** 2 3 4 5 6 7 **89** 5.0 (2.5)
Surgery					
Appropriateness	1 1 3 3 2 1 **1** 2 3 4 5 6 7 8 **9** 7.0 (1.1)ND	1 3 5 2 **1** 2 3 4 5 6 7 **89** 8.0 (0.6)ND	2 1 2 2 3 1 **1** 2 3 4 5 6 7 **89** 7.0 (1.4)ND	2 3 1 4 1 **1** 2 3 4 5 6 7 **89** 7.0 (1.2)ND	4 3 3 1 **1** 2 3 4 5 6 7 **89** 7.0 (0.8)ND

COMPREHENSIVENESS	AAOS	ACOEM	Intracorp	McKesson	ODG
Shoulder					
Physical Therapy					
Appropriateness	1 5 1 4 1 2 3 4 5 6 7 8 9 5.0 (1.4)	2 6 3 1 2 3 4 5 6 7 8 9 7.0 (0.5)ND	1 1 3 2 4 1 2 3 4 5 6 7 8 9 7.0 (1.7)ND	1 1 2 2 5 1 2 3 4 5 6 7 8 9 7.0 (1.2)ND	1 1 2 4 1 2 1 2 3 4 5 6 7 8 9 7.0 (1.5)ND
Quantity	1 3 2 3 1 1 1 2 3 4 5 6 7 8 9 3.0 (1.3)ND	1 2 3 3 2 1 2 3 4 5 6 7 8 9 5.0 (1.0)	1 2 2 4 2 1 2 3 4 5 6 7 8 9 7.0 (1.2)ND	1 4 3 3 1 2 3 4 5 6 7 8 9 7.0 (1.0)ND	1 1 2 4 3 1 2 3 4 5 6 7 8 9 7.0 (1.3)ND
Chiropractic					
Appropriateness	10 1 1 2 3 4 5 6 7 8 9 1.0 (0.5)ND	1 2 5 1 1 1 1 2 3 4 5 6 7 8 9 3.0 (0.9)ND	1 2 3 3 2 1 2 3 4 5 6 7 8 9 6.0 (1.0)	10 1 1 2 3 4 5 6 7 8 9 1.0 (0.4)ND	7 1 2 1 1 2 3 4 5 6 7 8 9 1.0 (0.8)ND
Quantity	10 1 1 2 3 4 5 6 7 8 9 1.0 (0.5)ND	5 2 2 1 1 1 2 3 4 5 6 7 8 9 2.0 (1.2)ND	1 1 5 2 2 1 2 3 4 5 6 7 8 9 7.0 (1.0)ND	10 1 1 2 3 4 5 6 7 8 9 1.0 (0.4)ND	9 1 1 1 2 3 4 5 6 7 8 9 1.0 (0.5)ND
Surgery					
Appropriateness	6 2 2 1 1 2 3 4 5 6 7 8 9 1.0 (1.1)ND	1 3 5 2 1 2 3 4 5 6 7 8 9 8.0 (0.9)ND	1 1 5 3 1 1 2 3 4 5 6 7 8 9 7.0 (0.9)ND	1 2 6 2 1 2 3 4 5 6 7 8 9 8.0 (0.5)ND	1 1 5 2 2 1 2 3 4 5 6 7 8 9 7.0 (1.0)ND

COMPREHENSIVENESS

	AAOS	ACOEM	Intracorp	McKesson	ODG
Residual Content	3 4 2 2	1 1 3 3 2 1	1 1 1 2 2 1 3	1 1 4 1 1 3	1 3 5 1 1
	1 2 3 4 5 6 7 8 9	1 2 3 4 5 6 7 8 9	1 2 3 4 5 6 7 8 9	1 2 3 4 5 6 7 8 9	1 2 3 4 5 6 7 8 9
	3.0 (1.5)ND	7.0 (1.2)ND	6.0 (1.6)	5.0 (1.5)	6.0 (1.0)
Entire Content	2 1 3 2 1 2	1 2 2 1 3 2	2 2 3 2 2	1 1 1 3 3 2	1 1 2 3 3 1
	1 2 3 4 5 6 7 8 9	1 2 3 4 5 6 7 8 9	1 2 3 4 5 6 7 8 9	1 2 3 4 5 6 7 8 9	1 2 3 4 5 6 7 8 9
	4.0 (1.4)	6.0 (1.5)	6.0 (1.3)	6.0 (1.2)	6.0 (1.1)

VALIDITY	AAOS	ACOEM	Intracorp	McKesson	ODG
Lumbar Spine					
Physical Therapy					
Appropriateness	1 _ 2 1 2 2 1 2 _ (1–9) 6.0 (1.7)	1 _ _ 1 2 2 2 3 (1–9) 6.0 (1.5)	2 1 3 1 2 1 1 _ _ (1–9) 4.0 (1.5)	1 1 _ 2 2 5 _ _ _ (1–9) 6.0 (1.3)	1 1 _ 4 2 1 1 1 _ (1–9) 5.0 (1.5)
Quantity	2 1 _ 2 2 _ 1 2 1 (1–9) 5.0 (2.3)	1 2 1 1 1 3 2 _ _ (1–9) 6.0 (1.8)	2 3 2 2 1 1 _ _ _ (1–9) 4.0 (1.3)	1 1 _ 2 6 1 _ _ _ (1–9) 6.0 (0.9)	2 _ 2 1 2 3 1 _ _ (1–9) 6.0 (1.6)
Chiropractic					
Appropriateness	5 2 2 1 _ _ _ 1 _ (1–9) 2.0 (1.4)ND	3 1 1 _ 4 _ _ _ _ (1–9) 5.0 (2.2)	1 2 4 _ 1 _ 4 _ _ (1–9) 2.0 (1.8)ND	1 1 1 1 3 1 2 1 _ (1–9) 5.0 (1.6)	1 1 _ 3 1 2 2 1 _ (1–9) 5.0 (1.7)
Quantity	6 1 1 2 _ _ _ 1 _ (1–9) 1.0 (1.5)ND	3 3 1 _ 1 2 _ _ _ (1–9) 3.0 (1.5)ND	3 3 1 2 1 1 _ _ _ (1–9) 2.0 (1.4)ND	1 1 1 1 1 4 2 _ _ (1–9) 6.0 (1.5)	1 _ 2 3 _ 3 2 _ _ (1–9) 4.0 (1.5)
Surgery-Decompression					
Appropriateness	_ _ _ _ _ 2 2 5 2 (1–9) 8.0 (0.7)ND	_ _ _ _ _ 1 6 2 2 (1–9) 7.0 (0.6)ND	1 1 3 2 1 3 _ _ _ (1–9) 5.0 (1.4)	_ _ _ _ _ 1 1 6 3 (1–9) 7.0 (0.9)ND	1 1 3 3 1 1 1 _ _ (1–9) 6.0 (1.3)
Surgery-Fusion					
Appropriateness	_ _ _ 1 3 1 4 2 _ (1–9) 8.0 (1.1)ND	2 5 2 1 1 _ _ _ _ (1–9) 6.0 (0.8)	2 4 2 2 1 _ _ _ _ (1–9) 3.0 (1.3)ND	1 2 _ 6 1 1 _ _ _ (1–9) 6.0 (0.9)	2 2 3 2 1 1 _ _ _ (1–9) 6.0 (1.2)

VALIDITY	AAOS	ACOEM	Intracorp	McKesson	ODG
Carpal Tunnel					
Physical Therapy					
Appropriateness	1 2 2 2 3 1 1 2 3 4 5 6 7 8 9 6.0 (1.7)	1 1 1 3 3 2 1 2 3 4 5 6 7 8 9 6.0 (1.4)	2 2 1 1 2 2 1 1 2 3 4 5 6 7 8 9 4.0 (1.8)	1 1 4 5 1 2 3 4 5 6 7 8 9 6.0 (1.0)	1 2 3 4 1 1 2 3 4 5 6 7 8 9 7.0 (1.3)ND
Quantity	2 2 3 2 1 2 3 4 5 6 7 8 9 3.0 (1.8)ND	2 4 2 2 1 1 2 3 4 5 6 7 8 9 2.0 (1.6)ND	1 4 4 1 1 1 2 3 4 5 6 7 8 9 4.0 (1.3)	1 2 1 1 5 1 1 2 3 4 5 6 7 8 9 6.0 (1.4)	1 1 1 5 2 1 1 2 3 4 5 6 7 8 9 5.0 (1.4)
Chiropractic					
Appropriateness	10 1 1 2 3 4 5 6 7 8 9 1.0 (0.5)ND	5 1 1 3 1 2 3 4 5 6 7 8 9 5.5 (1.6)	2 4 1 1 1 2 1 2 3 4 5 6 7 8 9 2.0 (1.5)ND	2 1 3 3 2 1 1 2 3 4 5 6 7 8 9 7.0 (2.0)ND	3 2 1 1 3 4 2 1 2 3 4 5 6 7 8 9 8.0 (1.5)ND
Quantity	10 1 1 2 3 4 5 6 7 8 9 1.0 (0.5)ND	1 1 1 2 3 3 1 2 3 4 5 6 7 8 9 8.0 (1.8)ND	2 5 2 2 1 2 3 4 5 6 7 8 9 2.0 (1.3)ND	2 1 1 1 5 1 5 1 2 3 4 5 6 7 8 9 8.0 (1.9)ND	1 5 1 1 2 2 1 2 3 4 5 6 7 8 9 5.0 (2.8)ND
Surgery					
Appropriateness	1 5 1 4 1 2 3 4 5 6 7 8 9 6.0 (0.9)	3 6 2 1 2 3 4 5 6 7 8 9 8.0 (0.5)ND	1 3 2 1 3 1 1 2 3 4 5 6 7 8 9 5.0 (1.4)	2 1 3 4 1 1 2 3 4 5 6 7 8 9 7.0 (1.0)ND	4 4 2 1 1 2 3 4 5 6 7 8 9 7.0 (0.7)ND

VALIDITY	AAOS	ACOEM	Intracorp	McKesson	ODG
Shoulder					
Physical Therapy					
Appropriateness	1 1 2 4 3 (1–9); 6.0 (1.1)	1 1 7 1 1 (1–9); 7.0 (0.6)ND	1 3 1 4 1 1 (1–9); 5.0 (1.3)	1 1 3 3 3 (1–9); 7.0 (1.2)ND	1 2 4 3 1 (1–9); 6.0 (1.0)
Quantity	2 3 1 1 2 1 1 (1–9); 3.0 (1.7)ND	1 1 3 3 3 (1–9); 7.0 (1.2)ND	1 3 1 3 3 (1–9); 5.0 (1.2)	1 1 6 2 1 (1–9); 6.0 (0.8)	1 1 2 5 2 (1–9); 7.0 (1.1)ND
Chiropractic					
Appropriateness	10 1 (1–9); 1.0 (0.5)ND	1 1 3 3 2 1 (1–9); 5.0 (1.8)	3 1 2 2 1 2 (1–9); 4.0 (1.9)	10 1 (1–9); 1.0 (0.4)ND	8 1 1 1 (1–9); 1.0 (0.8)ND
Quantity	10 1 (1–9); 1.0 (0.5)ND	5 2 1 1 2 (1–9); 2.0 (1.7)ND	2 2 3 3 1 (1–9); 4.0 (1.5)	10 1 (1–9); 1.0 (0.4)ND	10 1 (1–9); 1.0 (0.4)ND
Surgery					
Appropriateness	6 1 2 1 1 (1–9); 1.0 (1.4)ND	2 3 5 1 (1–9); 8.0 (0.7)ND	2 6 3 (1–9); 7.0 (0.6)ND	1 4 5 1 (1–9); 8.0 (0.9)ND	1 1 7 1 1 (1–9); 7.0 (0.5)ND

VALIDITY

	AAOS	ACOEM	Intracorp	McKesson	ODG
Residual Content					
(distribution over 1–9)	1 2 4 3	2 5 2 2	1 4 1 2 2 1	1 2 4 2 2	2 5 2 1
median (SD)	7.0 (1.5)ND	6.0 (1.1)	4.0 (1.4)	5.0 (1.2)	6.0 (1.0)
Entire Content					
Valid (distribution over 1–9)	2 2 4 1 2	1 3 1 1 5	2 4 1 1 2 1	1 2 2 2 2 2	2 1 5 1 1
median (SD)	7.0 (1.0)ND	7.0 (1.7)ND	3.0 (1.4)ND	6.0 (1.8)	6.0 (1.2)
Evidence-based (distribution over 1–9)	3 1 3 2 2	1 1 6 3	1 6 2 1 1	1 3 2 4 1	1 3 3 3
median (SD)	7.0 (1.2)ND	6.0 (0.6)	3.0 (1.1)ND	5.0 (1.1)	6.0 (1.1)

MEDIAN RANK					
	AAOS	ACOEM	Intracorp	McKesson	ODG
	3 1 6 5	5 4 1 1	2 1 1 3 4	1 4 2 3 1	3 1 6 1
	1 2 3 4 5	**1 2 3 4 5**	**1 2 3 4 5**	**1 2 3 4 5**	**1 2 3 4 5**
	5.0 (1.1)	2.0 (0.7)	4.0 (1.2)	3.0 (1.0)	3.0 (0.7)

Clinical Panelists' Comments

Regarding the quality of the five selected guideline sets as a group:

- Seven of the 11 panelists felt that the selected guidelines "are not as valid as everyone would want in a perfect world," that they "do not meet or exceed standards, they barely meet standards," and that "California could do a lot better by starting from scratch" and developing its own guidelines.
- Some panelists felt that if new guideline development were pursued, the existing guidelines would be a good starting point in the process. Input from specialty societies would also be valuable.
- One panelist advocated a patchwork of guidelines, while another favored a single guideline set.
- Individual panelists mentioned that the five guidelines are weak in discussing return to work, addressing practice patterns of use (especially for chiropractic manipulation and physical therapy), and specifying which type of surgeon can perform a particular procedure (e.g., guidelines instruct the provider to "refer to an orthopedist" and neglect other types of surgeons who may provide the same service).
- One panelist remarked that a scientific editor might be needed to make the guidelines more readable.

Regarding strengths and weaknesses of particular guideline sets:

- One panelist stated that the AAOS guideline was most helpful for orthopedic issues and the ACOEM was most helpful for other issues.
- One panelist remarked that the ODG guideline was not user-friendly, suggesting that it needed an index, as well as other changes.
- One panelist said that the downside of ACOEM is its focus on initial treatment.

- One panelist suggested that the ACOEM guidelines could be supplemented with additional specifics on physical modalities.
- Two panelists advocated using ACOEM together with ODG to address clinical and utilization issues.
- Four panelists noted having significant trouble accessing the McKesson guidelines online.
- Two or more panelists noted that the McKesson guidelines were organized in a way that made them very hard to understand.

Regarding proprietary utilization guidelines:

- One panelist felt that proscriptive guidelines (i.e., those designed for utilization management) might actually perpetuate inappropriate procedures by permitting them to be used despite a lack of evidence.
- One panelist worried about the potential expense of the proprietary guidelines.
- Three or four panelists reported preferring the clinical guidelines to the proprietary ones, which they find too "proscriptive," meaning the proprietary guidelines limit clinical options to a degree that makes these practitioners uncomfortable.

Regarding implementation policies:

- One panelist advised against having a given version of a guideline codified in the law or regulations, because major changes could be needed before updating would be possible.
- One panelist suggested a rapid approval system that would immediately approve care falling within the rules, thereby minimizing review hassles.
- One panelist stated that guidelines are often adopted as limitations, but they may not have been designed with this in mind. Therefore, this use is inappropriate.
- One panelist noted that a backup system should be implemented to monitor outcomes.
- Two panelists advocated early, even first, access to specialists, who are most knowledgeable and who can make correct diagnoses. The specialists can identify patients who would benefit from conservative management, avoiding the psychosocial problems that result from being labeled with an illness.
- Another panelist advocated early or first access to physical therapists, who may be able to treat a variety of common minor injuries.

- One panelist noted that prevention and early intervention warrant greater emphasis overall.
- One panelist noted that using rigid guidelines to restrict care might be short-sighted. Another noted that constraining medical care costs may increase indemnity costs and that it may be necessary to redesign the system.
- One panelist said that insurance companies currently using the ACOEM guidelines need a "bright line" to delineate appropriate from inappropriate care to avoid misinterpretation.
- Another panelist suggested having an expert panel oversee the implementation process to assist with interpretation issues.
- Another panelist responded that the California Industrial Medical Council was that type of an expert panel, and it was not successful.
- One panelist suggested that a local, hospital-based team might be used to review appropriate care.

Regarding guidelines not included among the selected five:

- One panelist suggested that the AHCPR back guideline could be updated because it addresses back injuries best.
- One panelist thought the Colorado guidelines were good and noted that they address only a few topics, including psychosocial issues.
- Another panelist recommended the Ontario, Canada, Association document because it addresses acute and chronic care well.

Regarding the RAND guideline evaluation method:

- One panelist thought the proprietary guidelines and the clinical guidelines are comparable, because some are good for providers to use, and others are good for case managers.
- Another panelist thought that having broad topics, such as surgery for shoulder injuries, is like asking someone to rate a whole guideline on chest pain. This panelist believes the literature should be used to develop specific recommendations for individual patients.
- A few panelists had a discussion over whether any high-quality clinical trials supported a particular treatment. They mentioned a few specific articles, and attempts were made to locate the articles on the Internet, but these attempts were unsuccessful. This reflects a limitation of the RAND panel process, which did not have adequate scope to include an exhaustive review of the literature.

Regarding physical modalities:

- Panelists providing physical modality services and those not providing such services described the relevant literature differently. Providers of physical modality services cited published literature for their specialties, and some physicians admitted being unfamiliar with that literature. Some physicians were also relatively unfamiliar with certain physical modalities, such as chiropractic manipulation of the wrist and shoulder. The chiropractors were aware of only two very small studies addressing chiropractic manipulation of the carpal tunnel. Panelists seemed to think quantity of care was also not addressed well by the literature.

Participants in the Stakeholder Meeting

Douglas Benner, MD
Coordinator, Occupational Health
Kaiser Permanente, NCAL
California Medical Association

Linda Botten, OTR/L
Member, Government Affairs Committee
Occupational Therapy Association of California

Carl Brakensiek, Executive Vice President
California Society of Industrial Medicine and Surgery

Steve Cattolica
Director of Government Relations
California Society of Physical Medicine and Rehabilitation

Rea Crane
Medical/Rehabilitation Director
California Workers' Compensation Institute

Mary Foto, OTR/L, FAOTA, CCM
Member, Third Party Reimbursement Committee
Occupational Therapy Association of California

Mark Gerlach
Applicants' Attorneys Association
California Applicants' Attorneys Association
Alejandro Katz
California State Oriental Medical Association

Michelle Lau
President
Council of Acupuncture and Oriental Medicine Associations

Mary King
California Self-Insurers Association (CSIA)

Elizabeth McNeil (via conference call)
California Medical Association
Director of Federal Issues and Workers' Compensation Advocacy

Ted Priebe
California State Oriental Medical Association

Diane Przepiorski
California Orthopedics Association

Jose Ruiz
Legislative and Regulatory Analysis and Implementation Supervisor
State Fund

Libby Sanchez (via conference call)
Law Office of Barry Broad

Alex Swedlow
Executive Vice-President/Research and Development
California Workers' Compensation Institute

Robert Thauer
President
The Alliance for Physical Therapy, Rehabilitation & Medical Technology

Thomas E. Tremble
Director, Government and Regional Affairs
AdvaMed

Willie Washington
Legislative Director, Workers' Compensation
California Manufacturers and Technology Association

Michael Weinper, MPH, PT
President
PTPN (California Physical Therapists)

Wayne M. Whalen, DC, DACAN
Former President
California Chiropractic Association
CCA Workers' Compensation Committee Member

Jim Zelko
Secretary/Treasurer, Kaiser Permanente
California Self-Insurers Association (CSIA)

Commission on Health and Safety and Workers' Compensation
    Christine Baker, Executive Officer
    Irina Nemirovsky
    Lachan Taylor, Staff Judge

Division of Workers' Compensation
    Anne Searcy, MD, Associate Medical Director
    Linda Pancho, JD, Legal Unit

The RAND Corporation
    Barbara Wynn, Co-Principal Investigator
    Teryl Nuckols Scott, Team Leader
    Yee-Wei Lim
    Rebecca Shaw
    Laura Zakaras

Stakeholder Discussion Questions on Guidelines Implementation Issues

1. Exceptions to the guidelines:
   - What is the appropriate balance between applying the guidelines and recognizing exceptions?
   - How might a policy addressing this issue be incorporated into the guidelines?

2. A single guideline set vs. multiple guidelines:
   - What are the tradeoffs between a single guideline set and a patchwork of multiple guidelines?
   - What are the most important considerations?

3. Topical gaps in the guidelines:
   - Who should have medical-necessity burden of proof when
     - Other evidence-based guidelines are available?
     - No evidence-based guidelines are available?
   - Would a hierarchy of evidence help?

4. Lack of relevant research:
   - What occurs when there is no research from which to generate evidence-based recommendations?
   - What should occur
     - For established treatment modalities?
     - For experimental or emerging technologies?
     - For unique circumstances?

5. Updating and implementing revised guidelines:
   - What are the operational and training issues involved in implementing guidelines?
   - How frequently should guidelines be updated?

Bibliography

Agency for Health Care Policy and Research (AHCPR), *The Outcome of Outcomes Research at AHCPR: Final Report, Summary*, AHCPR Publication No. 99-R044, available at http://www.ahrq.gov/clinic/ outcosum.htm, current as of September 1999.

The AGREE Collaboration, *Appraisal of Guidelines for Research and Evaluation, AGREE Instrument*, September 2001, available at http://www. agreecollaboration.org/instrument/.

American College of Occupational and Environmental Medicine Occupational Medicine Practice Guidelines, 2003.

Bauchner, H., and L. Simpson, "Specific Issues Related to Developing, Disseminating, and Implementing Pediatric Practice Guidelines for Physicians, Patients, Families, and Other Stakeholders," *Health Services Res*, 33(4 Pt. 2), 1998, pp. 1161–1177.

Burgers, J. S., B. Fervers, M. Haugh, M. Brouwers, G. Browman, T. Philip, and F. A. Cluzeau, "International Assessment of the Quality of Clinical Practice Guidelines in Oncology Using the Appraisal of Guidelines and Research and Evaluation Instrument," *J Clin Oncol*, 22(10), 2004, pp. 2000–2007.

California Workers' Compensation Institute, *Frequently Asked Questions*, available at http://www. cwci.org/faq, last accessed November 11, 2004.

California Workers' Compensation Institute, Policy News Current Issue, *Top 150 OMFS Procedure Codes in Calif. WC*, May 23, 2003, available at http://www.cwci.org/ newsroom/, last accessed November 5, 2004.

Campbell, D. T., and J. C. Stanley, *Experimental and Quasi-Experimental Designs for Research*, Boston: Houghton Mifflin Company, 2005 (reprinted from Virginia Richardson (ed.), *Handbook of Research on Teaching*, Boston: Houghton Mifflin Company, 1963).

Centers for Medicaid and Medicare Services, *Medicare Program Integrity Manual*, available at http://www.cms.gov/manuals/108_pim, last accessed 11/09/04.

The Cochrane Reviewers' Handbook Glossary, version 4.1.5, updated December 2003, available at http://www.cochrane.org/resources/handbook/ glossary.pdf.

Cohen, A. M., P. Z. Stavri, and W. R. Hersh. "A Categorization and Analysis of the Criticisms of Evidence-Based Medicine," *Int J Med Inform*, 73(1), February 2004, pp. 35–43.

Field, Marilyn J., and Kathleen N. Lohr (eds.), Committee to Advise the Public Health Service on Clinical Practice Guidelines, Institute of Medicine, *Clinical Practice Guidelines: Directions for a New Program*, Washington, DC: National Academies Press, 1990, available at http://books.nap.edu/books/0309043468/html/38.html#pagetop.

Coulter, I., A. Adams, and P. Shekelle, "Impact of Varying Panel Membership on Ratings of Appropriateness in Consensus Panels: A Comparison of a Multi- and Single Disciplinary Panel," *Health Serv Res*, 30(4), October 1995, pp. 577–591.

Davis, D. A., "Does CME Work? An Analysis of the Effect of Educational Activities on Physician Performance or Health Care Outcomes," *Intl J Psychiatry in Med*, 28(1), 1998, pp. 21–39.

Davis, D. A., and A. Taylor-Vaisey. "Translating Guidelines into Practice: A Systematic Review of Theoretic Concepts, Practical Experience and Research Evidence in the Adoption of Clinical Practice Guidelines," *Canadian Med Assn J*, 157(4), 1997, pp. 408–416.

Davis, D. A., M. Thomson, A. Oxman, and R. Haynes, "Changing Physician Performance: A Systematic Review of the Effect of Continuing Medical Education Strategies," *JAMA*, 274(9), 1995, pp. 700–705.

De Angelis, C., et al., "Clinical Trial Registration: A Statement from the International Committee of Medical Journal Editors," *New Engl J Med*, September 16, 2004.

Deyo, R. A., A. Nachemson, and S. K. Mirza, "Spinal-Fusion Surgery: The Case for Restraint," *N Engl J Med*, 350(7), February 12, 2004, pp. 722–726.

Eccleston, S., X. Zhao, and T. Liu, *The Anatomy of Workers' Compensation Medical Costs and Utilization: Trends and Interstate Comparisons*, 4th ed., Cambridge, MA: Workers Compensation Research Institute, 2004.

Ermann, D., "Hospital Utilization Review: Past Experience, Future Directions," *J Health Politics*, 13(4), 1988, pp. 683–696.

Feldstein, P., T. M. Wickizer, and J. R. Wheeler, "The Effects of Utilization Review Programs on Health Care Use and Expenditures," *N Engl J Med*, 318, 1988, pp. 1310–1314.

Fitch, K., S. J. Bernstein, M. D. Aguilar, B. Burnand, J. R. LaCalle, P. Lazaro, M. van het Loo, J. McDonnell, J. P. Vader, and J. P. Kahan, *The RAND/UCLA Appropriateness Method User's Manual*, Santa Monica, CA: RAND Corporation, 2001, available at http://www.rand.org/publications/MR/MR1269/.

Graham, I. D., S. Beardall, A. Carter, J. Tetroe, and B. Davies, "The State of the Science and Art of Practice Guideline Development Dissemination and Evaluation in Canada," *J Eval Clin Practice*, 9(2), 2003, pp. 195–202.

Grannemann, T. (ed.), *Review, Regulate, or Reform? What Works to Control Workers' Compensation Medical Costs*, Oylmpia, WA: Washington State Workers Compensation Research Institute, Washington State Department of Labor and Industries, 1994, available at http://www.lni.wa.gov/migration/ClaimsInsurance/Files/OMD/MedTreat/2002 MTGcomplete.pdf, last accessed November 12, 2004.

Gray, Bradford H., and Marilyn J. Field (eds.), Institute of Medicine, Division of Health Care Services, Committee on Utilization Management by Third Parties, *Controlling Costs and Changing Patient Care? The Role of Utilization Management,* Washington, DC: National Academies Press, 1989.

Grilli, R., and J. Lomas. "Evaluating the Message: The Relationship Between Compliance Rate and the Subject of a Practice Guideline," *Med Care,* 32, 1994, pp. 202–213.

Grimshaw, J. M., and I. Russell, "Effect of Clinical Guidelines on Medical Practice: A Systematic Review of Rigorous Evaluations," *Lancet,* 342, 1993, pp. 1317–1322.

Grimshaw, J. M., R. E. Thomas, G. MacLennan, et al., "Effectiveness and Efficiency of Guideline Dissemination and Implementation Strategies," *Health Technol Assess,* 8(6), 2004, pp. 1–72.

Grol, R., F. A. Cluzeau, and J. S. Burgers. "Clinical Practice Guidelines: Towards Better Quality Guidelines and Increased International Collaboration," *Br J Cancer,* 89, 2003 (suppl.), pp. S4–S8.

Grol, R., and J. Grimshaw, "Evidence-Based Implementation of Evidence-Based Medicine," *Joint Commission J Qual Improvement,* 25(10), 1999, pp. 503–513.

Harpole, L. H., M. J. Kelley, G. Schreiber, E. M. Toloza, J. Kolimaga, and D. C. McCrory, "Assessment of the Scope and Quality of Clinical Practice Guidelines in Lung Cancer," *Chest,* 123(1), 2003, pp. 7S–20S.

Hasenfeld, R., and P. G. Shekelle, "Is the Methodological Quality of Guidelines Declining in the U.S.? Comparison of the Quality of U.S. Agency for Health Care Policy and Research (AHCPR) Guidelines with Those Published Subsequently," *Qual Safety Health Care,* 12(6), December 2003, pp. 428–434.

Jones, G. W., and S. M. Sagar, "Evidence-Based Medicine: No Guidance Is Provided for Situations for Which Evidence Is Lacking," *Brit Med J,* 311(6999), July 22, 1995, p. 258; author reply, p. 259.

Khandker, R. K., and W. G. Manning, "Utilization Review Savings at the Micro Level," *Med Care,* 30(11), 1992, pp. 1043–1052.

Lipson, S. J., "Spinal-Fusion Surgery: Advances and Concerns," *N Engl J Med,* 350(7), February 12, 2004, pp. 643–644.

Lomas, J, G. Anderson, K. Domnick-Pierre, et al., "The Effect of a Consensus Statement on the Practice of Physicians," *N Engl J Med,* 321, 1989, pp. 1306–1311.

Matowe, L., C. Ramsay, J. Grimshaw, et al., "Effects of Mailed Dissemination of the Royal College of Radiology Guidelines on General Practitioner Referrals for Radiography: A Time-Series Analysis," *Clin Radiol,* 57(7), 2002, pp. 575–578.

Mays, G. P., G. Claxton, and J. White, "MarketWatch: Managed Care Rebound? Recent Changes in Health Plans' Cost Containment Strategies," *Health Affairs,* 23(4), 2004, pp. 287–296.

Meltzer, D., "Patent Protection for Medical Technologies: Why Some and Not Others?" *Lancet,* 351(9101), February 14, 1998, pp. 518–519.

Miles, A., P. Bentley, A. Polychronis, J. Grey, and C. Melchiorri, "Recent Developments in the Evidence-Based Healthcare Debate," *J Eval Clin Practice*, 7(2), May 2001, pp. 85–89.

National Guideline Clearinghouse Inclusion Criteria, available at http://www.guideline.gov/about/inclusion.aspx, last accessed July 2004.

Naylor, C. D., "Grey Zones of Clinical Practice: Some Limits to Evidence-Based Medicine," *Lancet*, 345(8953), April 1, 1995, pp. 840–842.

Park, R. E., A. Fink, R. H. Brook, et al., "Physician Ratings of Appropriate Indications for Three Procedures: Theoretical Indications vs Indications Used in Practice," *Am J Publ Health*, 79, 1989, pp. 445–447.

Rogers, E., "Lessons for Guidelines from the Diffusion of Innovations," *Joint Commission J Qual Improve*, 21, 1995, pp. 324–328.

Sackett, D. L., W. M. Rosenberg, J. A. Gray, R. B. Haynes, and W. S. Richardson, "Evidence-Based Medicine: What It Is and What It Isn't," *Brit Med J*, 312(7023), January 13, 1996, pp. 71–72.

Scheffler, R. M., S. D. Sullivan, and T. M. Ko, "The Impact of Blue Cross and Blue Shield Plan Utilization Management Programs, 1980–1988," *Inquiry*, 28(3), 1991, pp. 263–275.

Schlesinger, M. J., B. H. Gray, and K. M. Perreira, "Medical Professionalism Under Managed Care: The Pros and Cons of Utilization Review," *Health Affairs*, 16(1), January–February 1997, pp. 106–124.

Shaneyfelt, T. M., M. F. Mayo-Smith, and J. Rothwangl, "Are Guidelines Following Guidelines? The Methodological Quality of Clinical Practice Guidelines in the Peer-Reviewed Medical Literature," *JAMA*, 281(20), May 26, 1999, pp. 1900–1905.

Shekelle, P. G., "The Appropriateness Method," *Med Decision Making*, 24(2), March–April 2004, pp. 228–231.

Shekelle, P. G., M. R. Chassin, and R. E. Park, "Assessing the Predictive Validity of the RAND/UCLA Appropriateness Method Criteria for Performing Carotid Endarterectomy," *Int J Technol Assess Health Care*, 14(4), Fall 1998, pp. 707–727.

Shekelle, P. G., J. P. Kahan, S. J. Bernstein, L. L. Leape, C. J. Kamberg, and R. E. Park, "The Reproducibility of a Method to Identify the Overuse and Underuse of Medical Procedures," *N Engl J Med*, 338(26), June 25 1998, pp. 1888–1895.

Shekelle, P. G., E. Ortiz, S. Rhodes, S. C. Morton, M. P. Eccles, J. M. Grimshaw, and S. H. Woolf. "Validity of the Agency for Healthcare Research and Quality Clinical Practice Guidelines: How Quickly Do Guidelines Become Outdated?" *JAMA*, 286(12), September 26, 2001, pp. 1461–1467.

Smith, W., "Evidence for the Effectiveness of Techniques to Change Physician Behavior," *Chest*, 118(2), 2000, pp. 8S–17S.

Sohn, W., A. Ismail, and M. Tellez, "Efficacy of Educational Interventions Targeting Primary Care Providers' Practice Behaviors: An Overview of Published Systematic Reviews," *J Pub Health Dentistry*, 64(3), 2004, pp. 164–172.

State of California, Assembly Bill 749 (Calderon), *Workers' Compensation: Administration and Benefits,* February 19, 2002.

State of California, Board of Chiropractic Examiners, *Laws and Regulations Relating to the Practice of Chiropractic*, available at http://www.chiro.ca.gov/regulations/chiroregulations.mst.pdf, last accessed July 2004.

State of California, Code of Regulations, Title 8, Department of Industrial Relations, Chapter 1, Industrial Medical Council, available at http://www.dir.ca.gov, last accessed November 1, 2004.

State of California, Code of Regulations, Title 8, Department of Industrial Relations, Chapter 4.5, Division of Workers' Compensation, available at http://www.dir.ca.gov, last accessed November 1, 2004.

State of California, Labor Code Division 4, Workers' Compensation and Insurance, State of California, Department of Industrial Relations, California Code of Regulations, Title 8, available at http://www.legin.ca.gov, last accessed November 1, 2004.

State of California, Senate Bill 228 (Alarcón), *Workers' Compensation,* October 1, 2003.

State of California, Senate Bill 899 (Poochigan), *Workers' Compensation,* April 19, 2004.

State of Colorado, Department of Labor and Employment, Division of Workers' Compensation, Rule XVII, Exhibit A, "Low Back Pain Medical Treatment Guidelines, December 1, 2001," available at http://www.coworkforce.com/DWC/, last accessed November 1, 2004.

State of Washington, Administrative Code, Title 296: Department of Labor and Industries, Chapter 296-20, Medical Aid Rules, available at http://www.wa.gov/wac/index, last accessed November 9, 2004.

Telles, C., D. Wang, and R. Tanabe, *CompScope™ Benchmarks: Multistate Comparisons*, 4th ed., Cambridge, MA: Workers Compensation Research Institute, 2004.

Tobacman, J. K., I. U. Scott, S. Cyphert, and B. Zimmerman, "Reproducibility of Measures of Overuse of Cataract Surgery by Three Physician Panels," *Med Care*, 37(9), September 1999, pp. 937–945.

URAC, *The Utilization Management Guide*, 2d ed., Washington, DC: URAC/American Accreditation HealthCare Commission, 2000.

U.S. Department of Health and Human Services, Public Health Service, Agency for Health Care Policy Research, *Acute Pain Management: Operative or Medical Procedures and Trauma*, Rockville, MD: Agency for Health Care and Policy Research Publications, 1992.

Wensing, M., T. van der Weijden, and R. Grol, "Implementing Guidelines and Innovations in General Practice: Which Interventions Are Effective?" *Brit J Gen Practice*, 48, 1998, pp. 991–997.

West, S., V. King, T. S. Carey, K. Lohr, N. McKoy, S. Sutton, and L. Lux, *Systems to Rate the Strength of Scientific Evidence*, Evidence Report/Technology Assessment No. 47 (prepared by the Research Triangle Institute-University of North Carolina Evidence-based Practice Center under Contract No. 290-97-0011), Rockville, MD: Agency for

Healthcare Research and Quality, AHRQ Publication No. 02-E016, April 2002, available at http://www.ahrq.gov/clinic/epcindex.htm# methodology, last accessed November 1, 2004.

Wickizer, T. M., "Controlling Outpatient Medical Equipment Costs Through Utilization Management," *Med Care*, 33(4), 1995, pp. 383–391.

Wickizer, T. M., "The Effect of Utilization Review on Hospital Use and Expenditures: A Review of the Literature and an Update on Recent Findings," *Med Care Rev,* 47(3), 1990, pp. 327–363.

Wickizer, T. M., "Improving Methods to Identify Inappropriate Care: Targeting Strategies for Utilization Management," presented at the Annual Meeting of the American Public Health Association, November 2004, Washington, DC.

Wickizer, T. M., G. Franklin, J. Gluck, and D. Fulton-Kehoe, "Improving Quality Through Identifying Inappropriate Care: The Use of Guideline-based Utilization Review Protocols in the Washington State Workers' Compensation System," *J Occupational and Environmental Med,* 46(3), 2004, pp. 198–204.

Wickizer, T. M., G. Franklin, R. Plaeger-Brockway, and R. Mootz, "Improving the Quality of Occupational Health Care: The Washington State Occupational Health Services Project," *Milbank Quarterly,* 79, 2001, pp. 5–33.

Wickizer, T. M., and D. Lessler, "Utilization Management: Issues, Effects and Future Prospects," *Ann Rev Pub Health,* 23, 2002, pp. 233–254.

Wickizer, T. M., D. Lessler, and G. Franklin, "Controlling Workers' Compensation Medical Care Use and Costs through Utilization Management," *J Occupational and Environmental Med,* 41(8), 1999, pp. 625–631.

Wickizer, T. M., J. R. Wheeler, and P. Feldstein, "Does Utilization Review Reduce Unnecessary Hospital Care and Contain Costs?" *Med Care,* 27(6), 1989, pp. 632–647.

Williams, C., V. Reno, and J. Burton, Jr., "Workers' Compensation: Benefits, Coverage, and Costs, 2002," Washington, DC: National Academy of Social Insurance, 2004, available at http://www.nasi.org, last accessed November 1, 2004.

Wynn, Barbara O., *Adopting Medicare Fee Schedules: Considerations for the California Workers' Compensation Program*, Santa Monica, CA: RAND Corporation, MR-1776-ICJ, 2003.